LEGAL KIDNAPING

LEGAL KIDNAPING

*What Happens to a Family
When the Father
Kidnaps Two Children*

ANNA DEMETER

Introduction by Adrienne Rich

Beacon Press : Boston

Copyright © 1977 by Anna Demeter
Introduction copyright © 1977 by Beacon Press
Beacon Press books are published under the auspices
of the Unitarian Universalist Association
Published simultaneously in Canada by
Fitzhenry & Whiteside Limited, Toronto
Printed in the United States of America

(hardcover) 9 8 7 6 5 4 3 2 1

Grateful acknowledgment is made to the following:
Rosalie S. Sorrels, for permission to quote her
poem "Apple of My Eye" from *What, Woman, and Who,
Myself, I Am*, Rosalie S. Sorrels, ed. (Sonoma,
California: Wooden Shoe, 1974); and Susan Griffin,
for permission to quote from the third and fourth
stanzas of her poem "I Like to Think of Harriet
Tubman" from *Like the Iris of an Eye* by Susan Griffin,
copyright © 1976 by Susan Griffin.

Library of Congress Cataloging in Publication Data

Demeter, Anna.
   Legal kidnaping.
   Includes bibliographical references.
   1. Divorce — United States. 2. Custody of
children — United States. 3. Children's rights —
United States. 4. Children of divorced parents.
I. Title.
HQ834.D45   301.42'84   76-48502
ISBN 0-8070-2742-1

APPLE OF MY EYE

What can I say, but that it's not easy?
I cannot lift the stones out of your way,
And I can't cry your bitter tears for you.
I would if I could, what can I say?

But we're not one, we're worlds apart,
You and I,
Child of my body, bone of my bone,
Apple of my eye.

Like a young tree, I see you sway and bend,
And I'm so afraid, afraid you might break,
Tossed by the wind, the storms that come your way,
And careless strangers, seeing fruit, who reach out to take.

But we're not one, we're worlds apart,
You and I,
Child of my body, bone of my bone,
Apple of my eye.

I know my love must seem a distant thing to you,
For there's so many I must give it to,
But it will flow like a river to the sea,
And there'll be no end to it 'till there's an end to me.

But we're not one, we're worlds apart.
You and I,
Child of my body, bone of my bone,
Apple of my eye.

—Rosalie Sorrels

CONTENTS

ACKNOWLEDGMENTS

This book is for Alexander and Christopher. It is the story of how they were taken away, how Mommy cried, and how we all looked to find them. I owe thanks to many—family and friends— for love and immeasurable help through the living of these events and their telling in a book. Thanks go especially to Joanne Wyckoff and MaryAnn Lash of Beacon Press for patience and substantive assistance.

INTRODUCTION

In every life there are experiences, painful and at first disorienting, which by their very intensity throw a sudden floodlight on the ways we have been living, the forces that control our lives, the hypocrisies that have allowed us to collaborate with those forces, the harsh but liberating facts we have been enjoined from recognizing. Some people allow such illuminations only the brevity of a flash of sheet lightning, that throws a whole landscape into sharp relief, after which the darkness of denial closes in again. For others, these clarifications provide a motive and impulse toward a more enduring lucidity, a search for greater honesty, and for the recognition of larger issues of which our personal suffering is a symptom, a specific example. To try to understand what has been labeled the "personal," as part of a greater political reality, has been a critical process for feminism, more critical probably for feminism than for any other movement against oppression. For fundamental to women's oppression is the assumption that we as a group belong to the "private" sphere of the home, the hearth, the family, the sexual, the emotional, out of which men emerge as adults to act in the "public" arena of power—the "real" world—and to which they return for mothering, for access to female forms of intimacy, affection, and solace unavailable in the realm of male struggle and competition.

When women begin to think, speak, and write in ways which challenge these dichotomies, we meet a prevailing reflex of dread. It is not simply, I think, the dread of seeing a familiar model of

the world thrown into question, though this—the fear of potential change—is powerful enough. When we begin to describe
sexuality, motherhood, so-called "instinctual" or "natural" behavior, as part of the public world "out there"—that is, as affected
by power politics, rights, property, the institutionalized ownership
by men of women and children—we encounter acute anxiety on
the part of most men and many women. Even the recognition that
marriage is an economic institution—a recognition which was
perfectly clear to our ancestors well into the nineteenth century
—severely disturbs the contemporary, liberal, middle-class façade
of free choice, love and partnership, "liberated marriage," and
equality between the sexes in private life. The suggestion that
motherhood is not only a core human relationship but a political
institution, a keystone to the domination in every sphere of
women by men, evokes outcries of distress, or of vituperative
denial, from people with a heavy emotional and practical investment in leaving unexamined this "sacred calling." It is immediately assumed that the experience of maternity itself is under
fire, that the maternal emotions will be invalidated if we look
closely at the politics of motherhood.

The fear of change thus intersects with a fear that lucidity and
love cannot co-exist, that political awareness and personal intensity are contradictions, that consciousness must dissolve tenderness, intimacy, and loyalty. Lucidity, political awareness, and
consciousness are equated with intellectual nihilism, with deper-
sonalization, with a spirit of objectification. This is itself a measure
of the way in which Western culture in its intense patriarchal-
ism has polarized thought and feeling. In a society so dismembered, anonymous, and alienating, tenderness and intimacy are
precious and rare and—apart from all other forces which oppose
feminism—it is no wonder that people fear the loss of what
emotional intensity they still have. This book, written by a
woman who in her personal suffering chose lucidity and a political vision, demonstrates that this fear is a groundless one. It
suggests, in fact, that only when women recognize and name as
force and bondage what has been misnamed love or partnership,
can we begin to love and nurture out of strength and purpose

rather than out of self-annihilation and the protection of a crumbling form or fiction.

The significance of this book is much larger than its length and title might suggest. It was written to convert pain into something useful, and it has achieved that purpose to a remarkable degree. It is first of all the restrained yet highly charged account of the author's experience as a wife and mother, a wife seeking divorce and a mother whose two youngest children were kidnaped by her husband and held as hostages to force her back into the marriage. It uses that profoundly female, and feminist, genre, the journal, to carry the reader with Anna Demeter through the days and nights of her ordeal. It looks with courageous honesty at her earlier efforts to stay in a marriage which under a "gloss ...of new forms and new sensibilities" was quite traditional, filled with unspoken and unspeakable feelings, with denial, psychic violence, and sexual bargaining. Both spouses professionals, even colleagues; the husband taking some part in the care of the youngest child; the wife a feminist who defended "liberated" marriage on public platforms; her husband taking credit for having a "liberated" wife—this network of ironies and hypocrisies will seem unnervingly familiar to many readers, and it disabled Anna Demeter for some time from acknowledging her husband's destructiveness toward her children and herself. Proud, enormously competent, running a clinic, making speeches, baking the family bread, reading aloud nightly to the children, protective of her husband's reputation both as a father and as a professional, possessed by that "sense of privacy" which is so often the concealment of what conflicts with our self-image (and which so often cuts us off from understanding and help), believing that if she could only hold out till the children were grown she would have earned her freedom—many of us who have been characters in the fiction of a marriage can recognize ourselves in Anna Demeter, both our self-delusions and our incalculable strengths. Her passage on the "unfit mother" goes straight to the core of the experience of countless women. And I do not think I have seen rendered, even in poetry or fiction, the physical sensations of maternal longing as Anna Demeter describes them here.

Legal Kidnaping is also a kind of sourcebook for women who have to deal in their own lives with the law and the social order as they relate to parental kidnaping, specifically by the father. (This form of revenge for a proposed divorce action has become increasingly prevalent, so that many child-care centers and schools have established a "never-the-father" protocol, specifying who may and who may not pick up children after school; and legislation has recently been proposed to regularize custody and visitation among the states and to make parental kidnaping a federal crime.) In her Appendix, Anna Demeter has compiled concrete information, and a legal bibliography, based on her own experience and her research. Much of women's vulnerability as both wives and mothers comes from ignorance of the rights we have, of what recourse we can seek, and what legal power men have over us. For this information alone, Anna Demeter's book deserves a place in public libraries, legal clinics, women's centers, and the libraries of counselors and social workers dealing with women and divorce.

But finally, *Legal Kidnaping* is not a guide to one isolated problem, one exceptional aspect of divorce. In brief space, Anna Demeter raises very large questions about the institutionalization of human relationships, and about the entity called the family—that battleground, open wound, haven, and theater of the absurd, which dominates each human childhood. She attaches the issue of the rights of children to the questions feminism has raised about the possession of persons, about motherhood. The question "Mothering for what?" is essentially the question: "Into whose hands are we to deliver our children, whom are we training them to obey, and for whose benefit?" It is central to the feminist critique of all economic, sexual, cultural, familial relations as patriarchally controlled, and to the radical feminist demand for change in every aspect of the social order.

The mother-child relationship can be seen as the first relationship violated by patriarchy. Mother and child, as objects of possession by the fathers, are reduced both to pieces of property and to relationships in which men can feel in control, powerful, wherever else they may feel impotent. Legally, economically, and through unwritten sanctions, including the unlegislated male-bonding net-work documented in this book, the mother and her child live under male control although males assume a minimal direct re-sponsibility for children. Anna Demeter's discussion of the differ-ences between "mother-right" and "father-right" and between the institutionalized obligations of mothers and fathers toward chil-dren is a new step in the construction of a feminist theory of motherhood. The father's economic "obligation to support" allows him right of access to and contact with a child almost without regard to the kind of person he is; "mother-right" is legally the obligation to nurture and can be stripped from a woman on the grounds of her personal fitness as a mother.

Within the institution of patriarchal marriage, the following is true: A woman may be challenged with "unfitness" as a mother if she works outside the home and is thereby able to support her children (a threat to the economic basis of father-right). A woman who wishes to divorce her husband to marry another man is tol-erated more readily than a woman who leaves a marriage in order to be separate and self-sufficient, or because she finds marriage it-self an oppressive institution. An adopted child in a divorce settle-ment may be perceived as belonging only to the mother, while the biological child is regarded as the "seed" of the father. Thus motherhood is identified with nurture, fatherhood with the mo-ment of conception and with economic power. A husband's vilifi-cation of his wife, with the intention and possible effect of dam-aging her socially and professionally, is not legally considered slander. A man cannot be legally prosecuted for raping his wife. A man's obscene telephone calls to his wife are not legally action-able as obscene, nor can she have a tap put on her telephone to locate him. Paternal custody is often sought not out of desire for the children but as a weapon of vengeance against their mother. A majority of recent cases of parental kidnaping have been cases of kidnaping by fathers, in which the motive was to punish the mother and force her to return to the marriage. Such cases, unless a custody settlement has already been reached, are viewed as "private," a "marital dispute," and law enforcement agencies cannot be called into the search. Even where a custody settlement has been reached, the kidnaping of a child may be re-warded with a new custody hearing. The "preservation of the family" is quoted as an abstract principle without considering the quality of life within the family, or the fact that families may be held together by force, legally sanctioned terrorism, and the threat of violence.

"Father-right" must be seen as one specific form of the rights men are presumed to enjoy simply because of their gender: the "right" to the priority of male over female needs, to sexual and emotional services from women, to women's undivided attention in any and all situations. It would seem that a man experiences the violation of some profound "right" when a woman leaves him: the "right" to her services, however lacking in mutuality the re-lationship. Through patriarchal socialization, men learn to think in terms of their "rights" where rights are not actually the issue: in areas like sexual behavior, maternal behavior, which are seen, not as springing from a woman's choice and affections but as be-havior to which the male is entitled *as a male*. The husband's "rights" over his wife are, in social terms, all-inclusive; they can be whatever the man defines them to be at any given moment. The patriarchal legal system, with its more limited definition of rights of sexual access and of possession of children, interacts with and augments this much larger, more diffuse area of all-inclusive rights of men to the bodies, emotions, and services of women.

There is much in this book that points to the need for a new psychology of male behavior. A wife's declaration that she is about to seek divorce is a frequent occasion for a husband's violence, against others or himself, which has been latent or contained within the marriage. Anna Demeter suggests that a wife may be felt as a substitute for the lost mother, purchased through eco-nomic support and assured to a man by the institution of mar-riage. When a wife says she is leaving, many men are thrown back to the rage and anguish of separation from their mothers, less perhaps the "Oedipal" separation than through the fact that the mother is expected to hand her son over to the societal "fathers," to eject him from the female matrix, and allow him to become a "real man"—competitive, emotionally defended, prone to vio-

lence. Cast out from the female sphere once, he relives that anguish when a wife divorces him or a woman "turns him down."
Michael, the husband described in this book, was a visibly angry
and violent man who had suffered parental kidnaping himself as
a child. (Like child abuse, kidnaping may repeat itself from generation to generation.) But a man need not have lived through so
overt a drama in his childhood to act out primal rage and despair
when a woman seems to be depriving him of his one source of
nourishment—the maternal, female element. Because the family
has stood as the embodiment of maternal and female qualities,
absent in the male-dominated society at large, it carries an unholy
burden, beyond anything any actual family—or any single, actual
woman—can possibly provide.

Much male fear of feminism is the fear that, in becoming whole
human beings, women will cease to mother men, to provide the
breast, the lullaby, the continuous attention, associated by the infant with the mother. Much male fear of feminism is infantilism
—the longing to remain the mother's son, to possess a woman who
exists purely for him. These infantile needs of adult men for
women have been sentimentalized and romanticized long enough
as "love"; it is time to recognize them as arrested development,
and to re-examine the ideal of preservation of "the family" within
which those needs are allowed free rein even to the point of violence. Because the law and the economic and social order are
heavily weighted in favor of men, the infantile needs of adult
males are affirmed by a machinery of power which does not affirm
or validate the needs of adult women. Institutionalized marriage
and motherhood perpetuate the will of male infants as law in the
adult world.

This book will undoubtedly have an illuminating effect on
women contemplating divorce from physically violent men, or
men who seem capable of violence and kidnaping as retributory
measures. This is a larger male population than is usually acknowledged. It is essential that such women see themselves as the
breakers of a cycle of generational violence. It is essential for
women to realize, as Anna Demeter was finally able to realize,
that having acted as honestly and decently as possible we cannot

take on ourselves responsibility for a husband's disordered behavior on confronting divorce. Such assumption of total responsibility is part of the mother/child pattern in which so many
marriages are cast: the woman protecting the man at the expense
of her own and her children's selfhood and integrity; the woman
as responsible adult, the man as irresponsible child. As more and
more women refuse to be entrapped and mystified by institutional
marriage and motherhood, the less likely are new generations to
re-enact familial tragedy.

Beyond the issues of marriage and divorce, beyond the issue of
motherhood, lies the implacable political necessity for women to
gain control of our bodies and our lives. We must do this for ourselves and for each other; we can also believe that as we do so,
the generational sickness will repeat itself more and more rarely.
Clearly, Anna Demeter and her children have not been destroyed
by their ordeal but strengthened in their mutual bonds; her relationship with the world is clearer, more honest than it ever was;
her sense of integrity reconstituted through her refusal to give in
to terrorism. We do not "save" men by bending to violence, nor
do we "save" our children by letting them see, in their own homes
—their first community—violence prevailing as the ultimate recourse in human relations, and victimization accepted in the name
of "love." The children of mothers who are able to take their
lives in hand and confront the institutions that oppress them are
our best hope for a future in which human existence will no
longer be ruled by hypocrisy and force.

Adrienne Rich

FOREWORD

This is the story about an unexpected turn in the course of several lives bound together—a turn that highlighted, for me, the position of women and children as objects in their relationships to men. Set against the backdrop of a rather ordinary divorce, the events surrounding the kidnaping of my children, their prolonged and unreachable absence, and their return dramatized the contrast between father-right and mother-right as they are presently defined by laws, institutions, and public opinion.

The focus in the telling of this story is on the presumed and real rights of mothers. Other recent books and articles have drawn attention to the rights of fathers. There remains to be written (and before that, comprehended) an analysis of the rights of children. Men are speaking for men, and women for women, but young children cannot fully represent their own position in society. "Children's rights," until now, has often been a battlecry for patriarchal men, deeply opposed to that perspective on *human* rights called feminism. They have said, "If you think women have it bad, just look at children. If you women become preoccupied with your own condition you will only worsen the plight of children. What they need is more devoted mothering, not less." These men never address the question, "Mothering for what?" Are we women to care for our children *because* we are required to present them to the world of men, well-nourished, clean, neat, and trained to obey? This assumption underlies most current thinking about the rights of mothers as the responsible caretakers of children. I do not believe that the question of the rights of children can be comprehended until we more clearly understand the relationship between the rights of fathers and the rights of mothers.

Women are just learning the extent to which *we* are objectified, regarded as pieces of property, and owned by the men in our lives. That right of ownership exists in the minds of men, in our social conventions, in our laws, and in our expectations about ourselves. Unspoken rules lead everyone, including ourselves, to assume that we "belong to" one or more of the men in our lives. These rules are subtle and partially concealed by the pleasant fiction that adult women *can* be free and independent persons. Sometimes, as in my story, the rules become very explicit and obvious. Women have yet, however, to explore and understand the extent to which children are also regarded as objects, owned especially by their fathers. While mother-right in our society is essentially an obligation to bear, nurture, and care for our children on behalf of the men who are their *personal* fathers, we owe that obligation also to *societal* fathers, the patriarchs of industry, education, government, and so on, who need our children to become units in their plans and dreams. Father-right, in contrast to mother-right, is a guaranteed prerogative of access and claim, symbolized by the requirement that the child have the same surname as the father. The child will carry on for the father—seed, family line, reputation, and property ownership—if only the father admits the obligation to support, whether or not that obligation is fulfilled. Both mother-right and father-right, then, put the child in the position of an owned and cared-for object. Children have few if any rights as autonomous persons.

We women have colluded in this arrangement. We have pretended that it doesn't exist, taking part in marriage and motherhood with our minds, hearts, and souls so intent upon our own survival and our compelling need for affiliation that we only rarely allow ourselves to acknowledge the objectification of our children. Only at times in history—such as now—when women have collectively shared understanding and energy to try to change our positions as owned objects, have we begun to expand our conscious awareness to see the plight of our children.

The divorce of this story may seem somewhat more dramatic than most divorces. But the drama always centered on property rights, ownership of things and people. The issues, therefore, are typical of many, if not all, contemporary divorces. Divorce is, or can be, terrible. When divorce is terrible in its consequences, it seems to play out the profoundly painful constraints of marriage itself. Despite the liberalization of divorce law in recent years, divorce actions still reflect what is wrong with marriage; the solution contains the same biases, pitfalls, and dangers as the problem. Both Marriage and Divorce are institutions; Family is also an institution, and as such is controlled by the institutions of Marriage and Divorce. Only if "family" is seen as a group living together with a commitment to care can there be any hope of the family's escape from the property-ownership conventions of Marriage and Divorce. Throughout the divorce of this story I believed that that sort of family could and would survive for us.

The events described here are colored by the personalities, experiences, and occupations of the individuals involved. The two adult participants, especially, can be seen as peculiarly singular in childhood experiences, in their occupations as physicians, and in the idiosyncrasies of their personalities. I am convinced, however, that much of what happened is typical of the conventional relationships among women, men, and children. It is not at root an idiosyncratic story but a common story.

Its meaning—and the only purpose in its telling—lies in that commonality. Everyone—whether woman, man, or child—is diminished by the conventions that allow or encourage men to exercise rights of property ownership over their wives and children. The harms that fall upon women, men, and children as a result of these conventions are, of course, vastly different in degree and direction. My ultimate concern is with the well-being of all, of both sexes and every age. I must begin, however, with concern for those I understand best—women. This story is for Everywoman. If it sheds more light on women's lives as wives and mothers, I hope the light will also illuminate—and perhaps even lighten, in that other sense—the lives of children and men as well.

LEGAL KIDNAPING

PROLOGUE

I thought I had to make a gesture of suicide to resolve the problem of my marriage. The "problem" of my marriage was the marriage itself. In nineteen years of a mostly traditional marriage, contracted in the spirit of the 1950s, I had been chronically terrified of Michael's rage; most of all I was terrified of the rage I thought he would turn on me if I said that I did not want to live with him any longer. From the beginning I had felt that my legal alliance with him was irrevocable: when I became his wife I became a possession—one of his most valued—and as the possession of a rageful man I did not feel that divorce was a possible option for me.

My rejection of the possibility of divorce was suspect, for I had constructed too many reasons why I could not end this marriage. I believed that my parents would be hurt and angry if I became a divorcé I thought Michael needed me as his mainstay. In his own childhood he had been battered by his parents' long, drawn-out, and bitter divorce struggle. I knew how cheated he had felt by their prolonged and angry squabbling. They seemed unable to tear themselves apart enough to halt the tug-of-war that centered on the physical possession of their children. I knew also how perpetually bereft Michael had felt, as a child, of his mother's attention and understanding, and I believed that my steadiness with him represented the only real and seemingly permanent source of caring he had ever known. Together we had allowed each other to construct a way of living that seemed to preclude

1

divorce: I accumulated children, four all together, two born to me (the oldest and the youngest) and two adopted, while Michael accumulated things so avidly that we had lots of possessions, some debts, and no savings at all. We had created a set of ties that reinforced a marriage that had become a trap for me, and I think for Michael as well.

The marriage, traditional as it was, had a gloss, a public façade, of new forms and new sensibilities. Tradition was reflected in our shared assumption when we married that I would be entirely responsible for child care and housework. Michael was quietly resentful and acted put upon if my work—which was similar to his—sometimes kept me away from the family during hours when Michael was at home. As compensation Michael demanded and—with his rages and sulks—finally got full and unshared control of "our" money. At best, Michael as husband *granted* his wife a higher status than women usually enjoy. However, his assumption of the right to "liberate" me—a little bit, on his terms, when it suited his needs—was the most traditional marriage trap of all. Later, after I had asked for a divorce, Michael remarked to a friend of mine, "I can't understand Anna—I've always let her do almost anything she wanted!"

I have always been independent and competent in my own right. But my independence and competence were authentic only in those pieces of my life that were distant from the marriage bind. We met and married when I was a medical student and Michael a resident in cardiology. We both intended to work actively in our profession. I did work throughout the entire time of our marriage. Even when my children were born, I simply juggled my work schedule and managed with less free time, less sleep, rather than take a leave of absence. I achieved some eminence in my work and Michael openly enjoyed the reflected glow of the polish and value of his wife, his possession.

I greatly believed that my energies were well placed in my marriage, that we two could grow and change together. I also grew to understand the accepted concept of "woman's place" and the frustrating difficulties of living within the constraints of traditional marriage. I wanted to alter the patterns of the relationship that governed our marriage. Michael did in fact, in response to my urgings, take on increasing bits of the child-care responsibility and agreed in principle that he had some obligation to share in the chores of household maintenance. But I knew at heart that it was terribly difficult, perhaps impossible, to change the original contract implied at the time of our marriage. It is likely that I was trapped by my own childhood expectations of myself-as-wife. I do know that it has always been a central part of Michael's definition of himself that he *never* change. Even when he superficially agreed that we might try to conquer the inequities of the world outside our marriage by altering the balance of power in our relationship, we never made more than superficial changes in the original contract.

As a feminist and a professional expert on families, I found myself telling audiences that fathers could and even should act as care-taking parents, that marital partners could and should share the responsibilities of household maintenance (especially if both were also employed for family income) and that the traditional binds of marriage could be overcome with patience, good-will and tolerance. When speaking publicly, I would give reassuring examples of these new sensibilities from my own marriage, all the while becoming increasingly uncomfortable and guilty about the lie I was concocting. Clearly, these public reassurances were told in a manner that belied the fact that my children and I were at the mercy of Michael's willingness to let us be ourselves. I continued to believe in the possibility of equitable marriage. But the implication I gave of equity in my own marriage only added one more block—that of public image—to my avenue of escape, a divorce.

Michael's willingness to let the children and me be ourselves existed sometimes, when it suited his needs. My own costs were an unflagging sexual compliance, acceptance of and even forgiveness for his use of the children and me as objects of his childish and self-centered rages, and acquiescence to his money- and possession-hungry aspirations for our style of living. The costs to the children seemed to me to be much higher. Only two of the four children were regarded in anything like a positive light by

Michael. The oldest, Jason, a first-year university student in nearby Minneapolis, and the youngest, two-year-old Christopher, who were fathered by Michael in the biological sense, were, he believed, very much like him and like each other. While they thought that they were too often the targets of his temper, in fact he often overlooked things they did that would have enraged him and brought a swift and terrible retribution if they had been done by either of the other two. Visitors to our house who observed Michael's behavior with the children were stunned, both by Michael's rage and by his undisguised favoritism, and told me so.

I long ago despaired at his unwillingness to listen to the children, to hear what had happened from their perspective. I despaired at his chronic and untrammeled anger—he clearly believed that it was his proper right to react with instantaneous and unmodified fury when he was irritated. I think that for Michael those habits represented a confluence of personality, early experience and upbringing, his training and work as a cardiologist, and his maleness.

For all the children—and especially for twelve-year-old Mary and six-year-old Alex, the two for whom he had no particular reason for empathy, the two who were not his biologically—the effect of what they called his "screaming" was devastating. Severe anxiety has been described as being like a blow to the head, wiping out one's ability to reason, react, learn. I saw the children, time and time again, receive that kind of psychological blow, and found myself after the fact trying to patch them up, explaining that "Daddy was tired," that they could have acted differently (for almost always what they had done was something that they would eventually learn not to do), that they were not really "incredibly stupid" or hopelessly unacceptable.

Even now I scarcely have the self-respect to contemplate the costs to me of my marriage to Michael. I clearly remember, with a shudder, a meal we ate in a restaurant years ago. Unable to bear in public the screaming rages that Michael heaped on two-year-old Jason, I left the eyes and ears of the other diners to sit on the grass outside with Jason, both of us missing our dinner but grasping for peace and understanding while Michael finished his meal inside. I pondered then, and many times after that, how despicable I was to go to such lengths to protect Jason only because the setting was public, while I permitted—even tried to justify—the same kind of verbal and psychological abuse in the privacy of our home. Many times I told the children, with sick dread in the pit of my stomach, that Michael was tired because he worked so hard, that they must respect him, that they were not allowed to express their anger at him because that only made him rage all the more. I watched while little Jason created an imaginary friend (really an enemy/object) out of a green velvet pillow: he called the pillow "son" and heaped abuse, both screamings and beatings, to relieve his own tensions.

I never thought, nor do I now think, that Michael was a monster. Given the pattern of his own upbringing, his suspicious and volatile personality, his training and work as a cardiologist with the prerogative, or even the expectation, that he be angrily authoritarian, and the tacit approval given by men to men for the expression of violent anger, I found that sort of behavior on his part to be expected. Other husbands and fathers are equally rageful, and many are more physically violent than Michael.

But even if I did not have the strength to put an end to the pain that I witnessed daily in my children's lives, I felt, increasingly over the years, that it was intolerable for me to see it happen and to give even tacit approval. The other specific, unresolvable issue in the unhappiness of our marriage was our chronic financial tangle, a problem that Michael only allowed me to glimpse at intervals. Michael's measure of his own goodness was in the things he owned. I have long believed that ownership is the prime meaning of his four children for him. Again, his gratification in things owned is common in the world of men—at least for men of a certain social class and experience—and I think Michael's behavior in this regard is only a little extreme, compounded of his childhood of deprivation and his present access to very high earnings.

Purchasing is his primary pleasurable passion. Even when he was depressed about his income and wished that he had more money to spend, he found comfort in buying things, using money already committed for necessities and driving us more and more into debt. It took years for me to understand that his depressions (which always increased his ragefulness) were almost always a reflection of a lack of pocket money and were quite unrelated to anything that I did or didn't do—except when I infuriated him by reciting proverbs from my childhood, like "we ought not to spend money that we don't have." His grumbliness and increased irritability at the children and at me were ultimately relieved—in the short run—by buying more expensive stuff, by borrowing more money, by defaulting temporarily on bills like school tuition. Our home took on the character of a very expensive junk heap: more and more things, costly but uncared-for, ultimately kicked aside, never thrown away, and replaced by even more expensive versions of themselves.

In this area, too, I could more easily think about the harm done to the children than I could become angry in my own defense. I feared for what the children were learning about the uses and values of money and about materialistic hoarding. I feared for their security since we seemed chronically to be in jeopardy of a very expensive disaster. I was tied in to those present and impending disasters by collusion with Michael's determined insistence that only he keep the books, have access to the information that would reveal the whole picture of our financial situation, and make decisions about purchases. My income went for the necessities of milk and heat and telephones and so on, enabling him to control whatever resources we had that were "optional." He would sometimes ask "Should I buy a ——?" I would counter with "Can we afford it; what *is* our current situation?" and he would reply "Of course we can afford it!" I would know that consulting with me had been only a formality. The few times I said that I didn't think we needed some costly and unnecessary object were held against me for years and ultimately became part of Michael's charge that I didn't care about the "welfare of our family."

I thought about running away, disappearing, losing my identity as a physician so that I could not be found, leaving my children behind. That seemed to me to be even more painful than the thought of suicide. I considered running away and taking the children with me. That was a fantasy that I could never cast in terms of reality. I imagined that I would have to live as a fugitive, move from one place to another, and be constantly pursued and harassed by the police and anyone else Michael might enlist to retrieve his possessions. My thoughts about divorce through all those years were only fleeting; knowing what grief Michael's parents had caused each other, knowing Michael's penchant for holding grudges and exacting retribution when he thought he had been wronged, knowing his capacity for psychologically violent rage, I was terrified. In my head, I heaped on reason after reason why a divorce was impossible for me. I hoped, wished that Michael himself would decide that our marriage was intolerable for him and would ask for a divorce.

Over the years of my married life, I learned about the joys of female friendship—a kind of personal involvement that I had been discouraged from wanting or pursuing for most of my life, as is true for most women. I had come to have many friends as the consciousness of the women's movement brought me into a sisterhood of strong, competent, caring women. I began to acquire an enduring sense of self-respect in the reflections of other women. I reassessed my womanliness as a worker and as a person, my socialization as a professional, the related invitation to join the role of "honorary man," and the intense and conflicting meanings of my motherhood.

Six months before my suicide gesture, our family moved to a new town, with new jobs for both of us, and what seemed to be a particularly good working and living situation for Michael. The move meant for me a separation from the physical nearness of friends, a loss I thought I was prepared to cope with. There was for me a sense of clearing the decks of dissatisfactions and distractions, of setting a stage to create the most beneficent family living situation for the next sixteen years of the children's lives, until Chrissy was grown and launched.

In the following six months the marriage disintegrated significantly. Despite my steady attention and energy, focused on easing the children's daily lives, the climate of our house became tighter and more unhappy. In what I can only understand as a midlife crisis, the move seemed to precipitate for Michael an intensification of his money passion. I only learned after the fact the full extent of our indebtedness. What I saw was his unremitting gloom, his passive withdrawal from the pleasantries of day-to-day living, his increasingly frequent and precipitously intensified rages at the children and at me. As had always been the case, he denied his moods of depression and anger; I truly believe that Michael, like many men, does not know when he is possessed by emotion and cannot contemplate such possession as anything but unmanly, unacceptable, dangerous.

I began to try to devise ways for me to survive as a person and still live in that house as Michael's wife. I tried for a while to pretend that I had a second job, in addition to my professional work —which was, as always, deeply gratifying. I imagined that I worked in that house as Michael's housekeeper/prostitute in return for room and board and the pleasures of being with and caring for the children. I thought again of running away by myself and of running away with the children. I tried to imagine that the children and I lived in that house without him, that he was an occasional foreign presence to be tolerated but not to be taken seriously. My panic rose.

I began to think seriously, for the first time, about divorce. When I thought through the matter carefully, to my fear of his massive, angry, and vindictive retribution, I was as trapped by fear as was any wife trapped by the expectation of a physical beating. I began to wonder whether there could be one last terrible psychological beating and then an end. Could our lives really be separated by divorce, or would Michael's anger pursue me until the children were grown or perhaps for all of my life? I heard many tales of vindictive former husbands, still possessed by rage years after a divorce.

I read, listened to lawyers, talked to friends. I began to flirt with the pretense that we could devise an "ordinary" divorce, painful in the separation but following the conventional rules: I would have custody of the children because I knew them best and they were closest to me; Michael would pay little or no child support after the first few months; he would take all of our property except for the house that we lived in; he would find another woman and a new life; he would visit with the children and might even grow in patience and tolerance with them once he was disconnected from me. For my own part, I would be content to invest myself in caring for my children, in my work, and in my friends. I could not envision investing myself again in the potential miseries of an intimate relationship until I had lived through a resolution of my entrapment with Michael. I was willing to understand that I was as difficult for Michael to live with as he was for me. But whenever I tried to believe that an ordinary divorce could be reached as a reasonable solution to our dilemma, I withdrew in the face of my intuitive fear that Michael would not agree to any ordinary divorce and would in fact put all of his considerable will toward punishing me, perhaps even with a willingness to hurt the children along the way.

As we avoided each other more and more and were less and less able to talk about our accumulated grievances, Michael himself began to suggest divorce, intending, I think, to threaten me back into smiling compliance. I suspect he believed that I would do anything to avoid a divorce. I held my breath. I hoped that he had found another woman.

As I began to probe his intent and determination to seek a divorce, he suddenly withdrew the offer. After that brief glimpse of blue sky, freedom from the unhappiness of living with him, and a resolution satisfactory to him because it was in his control, I felt as though my prison door had been slammed shut. I was his possession and no matter how angry he might be with me he would never let me go, no more than he could bring himself to sell the houses that we had once lived in. I felt as if my trap were now set for the next sixteen years.

Later, after the suicide gesture, I began to understand some of the complexities of the origins and meanings of that act. At one level I told myself—in a fit of terrible depression that seemed both urgent and beyond the helping hands of friends—that my life was intolerable, that I was weary of my efforts to cope, that a swift end was my only choice because all other solutions filled me with more fear and dread than the simple act of killing myself. At another level I needed to prove to myself, and to anyone watching (including Michael), that I would rather be dead than to continue as his wife: evidence that I had tried in every way I could to sustain the marriage. If Michael might be hurt by my demand for a divorce, and if in another way that demand put the children at risk of hurt in consequence of Michael's vindictive retribution toward me, then I needed to say "I would sooner be dead than continue in this marriage. I do not make this decision lightly, I am not frivolously asking for a self-indulgent kind of freedom, this *is* a life-and-death matter for me." At still another level I needed to say to Michael, out of my own anger, "I believe that you would almost rather see me dead than not loving you, not in your possession. Perhaps I can present you with that choice, and you can tell me which you would choose." And, finally, I could resolve my own indecision about whether I had the strength to endure what I so deeply feared, Michael's anger about a divorce, by tossing a coin to the Fates: if I died I would avoid the awful responsibility of starting a divorce, and if I did not die then I would take that as a sign that I must proceed with a divorce.

I left only a brief note, posted in the mail to the women I worked with—who would, I thought, understand what I believed I had to do. I took an assortment of drugs from my office, in sufficient quantities to do in a healthy young adult. I drove my car up a dark path off a secluded road. I was clumsy-fingered and very, very scared, but I finally got into my body what I thought was enough poison to do me in. Six hours later I woke up, first just knowing where I was (and how cold) and then gradually realizing that I had to go back. I was very unsteady, driving in the dark of the early morning, and very frightened of the repercussions of what I had done. I went home to Michael.

Michael was shocked. When I began to pour out my unhappiness about our marriage, he was very angry at me in his abrupt, tight-lipped fashion. He put me to bed and left me alone; in an hour or so he returned to say that no one must know about what I had done. Except for the three friends at work, who had re-

ceived my letter, I told no one and colluded in his plea for
secrecy. Although I did not understand it then, I thereby undid
much of the effect of what I had done in that terrible act. We
could almost pretend that it had not happened, that I had not
felt so desperate, that my pain and need were not so great.

I was sleepy and shaky, unable to pursue my request for a
divorce in the face of his tight-lipped anger. He left me alone,
reappearing now and then to loom over my fitful sleep. My courage failed quickly and with it the will to explain why I had
done what I felt I must do. I could only find the strength to
say to Michael that if I were to stay in the marriage I needed
more separation, more space. I asked for the privacy of a bedroom of my own and proceeded to return to work and to my
ordinary life, trying to keep some formal distance between Michael's life and mine.

Michael became absorbed in buying for Christmas. I knew
later that he had heard some of what I said that morning of
my suicide gesture. He began to talk about me to nurses, other
doctors, and even to his patients, as a neglectful mother, a slov-
enly housekeeper, an unsatisfactory wife.

At home he began a campaign of quiet watching. He investigated my affairs in ways that he had never done: reading my
mail, listening in on telephone conversations, asking what I was
thinking. He took and kept my appointment book for the year
just ending, although I did not know that until much later. I
did not think that any of my business was secret—years before
I would have been glad if he had interested himself in my life.
But I felt as if he were also prying himself into my head, hound-
ing me and spying.

One night we sat at the dinner table with the television on.
In a news item a "baby quieting" device was described—a record
of a pregnant woman's heartbeat and a rhythmic slosh that was
a magnification of the sound environment inside the pregnant
uterus. It seemed to me to be yet another electronic substitution
for mothering, a technological replacement for the naked com-
forts of skin-to-skin contact between mother and infant. The
male scientists who described this marvel did not point out that

their evidence supported the comforting effects of an almost instinctive kind of mother care for tiny babies. They were instead
delighted that no one had to hold a baby to provide those com-
forts, that they had devised yet another machine to substitute
for a mother. I remembered hearing male physicians describe
the mechanical-electronic equipment in a newborn intensive care
unit in a specialized hospital as "better than" a uterus; they saw
themselves as capable of replacing and improving on the natural
womanly processes that nurture babies before they are ready to
be born.

I listened to the news intently, reflecting on that universal male
jealously about the birthing capacity. In times past I might have
commented lightly and gently to the children, if any of them
seemed interested; Michael himself would never have wanted to
talk about such matters. This night he asked why I was interested
in that part of the news, and knowing his intent to invade my
thinking and to record his disapproval of me, I did not want to
talk about it. He harassed and harangued until finally I left the
table, tense and defiant. I realized then how our home had become a battleground, and how hard I was fighting to preserve
my integrity and intactness.

I felt that no one knew how desperate I was. In all the years
of unhappiness with Michael I had never talked about our relationship with my friends, feeling that to be a violation of our
contract. Now I felt as if my open plea for talk—the suicide
gesture—had been turned away, in part by Michael's insistence
and in part by my own fear. Even my good friends at work
avoided the topic of my suicide gesture.

Michael badgered me about my separate bedroom. He said
that he could tolerate almost any other kind of separation but
that having sex was what marriage was all about for him. I wondered whether if I held firm on that one issue he would again
begin to talk about a divorce. And yet, in angry response to what
had become an endless badgering conversation, I came to his
bed on his birthday, feeling even more like a prostitute than I
had felt in the last several years. Hoping still for some resolution
other than a divorce, I tried to salvage what I could out of that

piece of our bitter conflict by coming to him on my own initiative.

I believe that Michael, like many men, attributed to the act of sexual intercourse a level of emotional communication that satisfied his rather meager need for that sort of exchange. There was never any other place in our relationship in which he was expressive of need, yearning, tenderness. He could not identify and talk about his own feelings, nor mine, nor the children's. At the same time he used our sexual contact as a primary area for the acting out of issues of power, dominion, control. Despite his occasional verbal statements about a wish for mutuality in sex, his approach to me was always overburdened by his need to control me, to do to me, to play me like an object.

I could never trust his intent to create a sexual relationship of mutuality, in the face of his unwillingness or inability to deal with our unresolved difficulties about feeling and control in all the other areas of our life. Our long-standing disagreement about sex always came down to this: he proposed that if we could only work out an agreeable sexual relationship (by which he meant that he was satisfied, and that I communicated clearly that I was satisfied by him—his needs and performance being central to both sides of the exchange) then he would be willing to work on other aspects of our relationship—social, communicative, expressive, sharing. I, on the other hand, found myself paralyzed by what I experienced as a perpetual position of exploitation and domination. I could not begin to address myself to the tangles of our unsatisfactory sexual relationship until we could address the problems of all the other parts of our lives together.

Coming to his bed on his birthday, submitting to him with no pretense of enjoyment, not even that pale enjoyment of the past of "doing for him," showed me what I had let myself become. I remembered a young woman I had met in a counseling situation years before, promiscuous by the standards of my generation, who explained with a look of puzzlement, "but I would never go to bed with a man that I couldn't talk with!" It was too bad, I thought, that I didn't even have that much self-esteem.

Despite my controlled effort to work out some distanced relationship between us, I felt more and more sick at the charade.

At least every other day Michael would ask when I intended to return to his bed and to an ongoing sexual relationship. I was puzzled then and many times in the succeeding months that he would accept the most grievous and unhuman relationship between us, rather than relinquish his ownership of me. He acted then as if my request for a separation-in-the-same-house was a kind of temporary and unreasonable craziness with which he would be briefly and tentatively patient. I sensed that at some later time I would be forced to repay the debt that his "patience" with me was engendering.

I learned later that Michael had then begun a campaign to justify himself as long-suffering and exemplary and to paint me publicly as intolerably inadequate as a wife and mother. In the wards of the hospital and in social gatherings he began to describe me as neglectful of my children, of our home, and of him. He spoke of me as eccentric and politically irrational if not dangerous. One of his proclamations, said loudly in the presence of nurses, doctors, and patients in the hospital, catches the flavor: "I may be the one who has the penis, but I still have to be the mother in that family!" In his own worry and anxiety he stopped bathing and changing clothes every day and began to have the rumpled, unkempt look of a man whose wife is neglecting him.

In the small town where we were living, where neither of us was personally well known, his remarks laid the ground for a long-lasting and juicy scandal. I began to experience a kind of social isolation that further drained me. I had always had cordial and cheerful acquaintanceship with almost everyone with whom I came in contact. I now began to experience backs turned, people who would no longer acknowledge my presence in a room or on the street, failures to return my casual greetings. Small wonder—Michael had been busy announcing that I was dangerous, unstable, perhaps harmful to my children. This distance and uneasiness on the part of others added to my own sense of displacement from a world of reason and predictability.

I ate little, vomited chronically, and developed severe headaches. In the five weeks since I had made the suicide gesture, my life had taken on a flavor of insanity: I knew that I could no longer live with Michael; I feared what he would do if I demanded a divorce; I tried to find a way to coexist with him, and he was saying that he would simultaneously hold on and despise me.

I talked to a lawyer about my wish for a divorce. Paul, who had been recommended by a friend, suggested that he and I meet at the courthouse where he had a case and talk during lunch hour, an accommodation to my own work schedule. He listened only briefly—the problem was old and familiar to him—and told me that when people talked about their marriages as I was talking they almost always went through with a divorce.

I verbalized for the first time what I had been holding in, not even fully acknowledging to myself—my fear of Michael's retaliation. I said that I believed I represented to Michael a very important possession, both as an object and as a relationship of power and control. Loss of that possession would be personally infuriating and demeaning. If he lost that possession by the action of the object itself (thus, finally, turning around his dominion over me) he would, I believed, act out his anger in frightening and dangerous ways that I could not foresee but deeply feared.

Paul was smoothly professional and soothing. He reassured me that there were established legal processes to ease us through any complications that Michael might create. What did I fear? I stumbled, not even wanting to put a name to my apprehensions. Could I lose our home? Mothers and children customarily stayed in their family homes; since I did not want to claim any of our other property, Paul did not believe that that would be a problem. Could Michael so slander me in our town that I could not sustain my medical practice? Paul thought that as the divorce proceeded and came to an end Michael's temporary verbal violence would cease. Could I lose the children? Paul reassured me that he thought that improbable, if not impossible.

At that point I began to cope with my fears, now in the open, and with my own ever-ready sense of guilt. Socialized as a nice, middle-class girl by threats of loss of parental love—or, more accurately, by the warning that I would deserve love and ap-

proval only when and if I measured up to some seemingly unattainable standard of goodness—I was always ready to assume
that I was responsible for not averting anything bad that happened to me or to others around me. If Michael reacted to a
divorce with gigantic, momentous anger and, for instance, harmed
the children in the playing out of his anger, would I then feel
responsible and be forever pursued by my own self-imposed guilt?
My own personal, lifelong devil thus came to confront me. It
was only much later, when Michael's anger was in fact acted out
and I faced the wounds that he inflicted on himself, the children,
my friends, my parents, and me, that I understood what important work I had begun by confronting that devil and learning
that there were reasonable and rational limits to my responsibility
for Michael's actions.

My old friend Janet, a frequent visitor in our house, came to
visit. We talked about my despair, the need to tell Michael about
my intent to divorce him, and my fears. She offered to sit with
me, as a "public witness," when I told him of my intentions. We
three talked for an hour. Michael reacted with quiet hostility.
He threatened to make the fight as ugly, as bitter, and as punishing to me as he could. I realized later that that meeting of
about an hour was, for me, the real end of the marriage. Once
I said in the presence of a witness that it was over, it felt irrev-
ocably closed.

Janet urged that we visit divorce counselors, especially as she
observed Michael's anger. I agreed. I felt that it was important
for Michael and also for me that we talk, in some safe and supervised place, about how we had come to this point and where we
were going from here. My hope was that if we took some time
now, as the divorce began to get under way, we could work
out a civilized settlement and Michael could begin the process
of constructing a new life for himself. Having determined that
I would go through with a divorce, I wanted to believe that
there was a way to work matters through and minimize our pain.
I thought that since I only wanted our house for the children
to live in and none of our other property, and since I hoped
that we would continue to live in the same town and share in

our concern for the welfare of the children, we could sustain our family attachments even after the marriage was ended. I hoped that Michael could better begin to see the children as people—not as things that he owned—after his relationship and closeness to me had been broken. I was determined to be giving, in time and space, so that I could feel I had proceeded in the most thoughtful, the least hurtful manner. I wanted to prove that my fears of Michael's vindictive retribution were foolish and overwrought.

When I told Paul, early the following week, of our decision to see divorce counselors he advised against it, advice based on my description of Michael's usual behavior. He observed that in his experience Michael's personal reconstruction would have to be done by Michael after the divorce was over, and that the process of the divorce was bound to be a rageful time for a man like him. He described to me the reaction of other clients, men who got drunk and forced their way in to beat their wives or smash furniture.

From the beginning of our four weekly sessions with the divorce counselors Michael focused on two issues: either we would reconcile or he would struggle to take the children away from me altogether. The counselors quickly pinpointed a core issue in our relationship—Michael was either chronically angry or ready to be angry, and I quite simply never knew how to deal with his anger, vacillating between fearful acquiescence and scuttling little forays expressive of my own anger and resentment. There was also some discussion of my habitual stance as Michael's soother and protector, very evident to the counselors as we talked. In the last of our four sessions there were questions about our financial status, and Michael suddenly sank into surly privacy.

With Paul urging me to get on with the legal negotiations, I agreed with Michael when he suggested after the fourth counseling session that we were not accomplishing very much and should discontinue those meetings. Michael still did not have a lawyer. He had discussed in the last counseling session his consultation with a well-known, out-of-state attorney who had just won a much publicized case involving disputed custody—he and his client, the father, won that case and the mother lost custody.

Every time the question of custody came up I felt sick. I had invested so much energy, during all the years of the marriage, in teaching Michael how to spend time with the children, encouraging him to become an equal parent. With the last child, Christopher, he had become a skilled and happy baby tender, although he had never taken on anything like half of Chrissy's care. And since his dealings with the children past the years of infancy were one reason for my insistence on a divorce, I was heartsick at the very thought that he might try to keep me from them. I spoke with many people who had spent hours in our house and knew the quality of the children's relationship with each parent and was told time and again that I must fight for their custody, that they needed to live with me as their primary parent, that I was not just reacting out of my own need to care for them.

In all the years of our marriage Michael had expressed pride and pleasure at my relationship with the children. He was proud also of my work and said, both publicly and privately, that my work enhanced my mothering. Now, suddenly, he had turned to the claim that because I had worked *and* found satisfaction in my work I could not possibly be a good mother. It seemed unbelievable to me, something like a fantastic nightmare, that there could be any possibility that I would not continue to care for the children. Was it possible that anyone would believe Michael's ravings that he and not I had taken care of them for the past eighteen years?

On Paul's advice I consulted with a psychiatrist and submitted to a formal examination with regard to my apparent competence as a mother and specifically with regard to the suicide gesture. The psychiatrist said at the conclusion of his examination that he felt confident that my despair reflected my acute sense of entrapment in an untenable situation and did not signify either a significant psychological instability or a lack of fitness as a mother.

Paul told me, as Michael finally arranged to meet with his newly hired attorney, Paul, and me, that Michael had hired an attorney who was honest, straightforward, and a traditionalist as far as family relationships were concerned. That attorney met with Paul before our first joint meeting and told Paul that Michael was claiming that I was never at home, that I neglected the children, and that I was a feminist and possibly even a lesbian. The last accusation was breathtaking; I didn't realize then that Michael was probing for any or all of the traditional reasons for which judges decide that mothers cannot have custody of their children.

We spent two long afternoons negotiating. On the second afternoon I waited in another room, since my presence only inflamed Michael. At the end of the second day we had an agreement that both attorneys thought was reasonable and fair and something that Michael might sign. I agreed to every-other-day visitation with Michael for the two little boys, against my judgment, but hoping—as Paul suggested—that the judge would forbid such a torn-apart schedule for children of two and six. I also believed that Michael would discover in time that he didn't want that much child-care responsibility, more than he had ever had while we were married.

Paul said that he believed, and Michael's attorney believed, that Michael would sign the agreement we had talked about, given a few days to think it over. He advised that Michael not be served with divorce papers until after the agreement was signed—"being served with the actual papers is often something of a shock and makes men do irrational things." We were to regret that decision in a few days.

Paul also felt that our family finances were much more complicated than Michael was representing and that the present agreement had a virtue of simplicity, leaving Michael the complications that Paul was sure were there but that Michael wouldn't admit to. We simply divided down the middle all the assets and all the debts that Michael said we had, ignoring the fact that Michael's income as a cardiologist was about three times my income as a family practitioner. My share of that division-in-half was the house that we now lived in, conforming to the usual divorce practice of leaving the mother and children in their own home. Michael was free to arrange the rest as he preferred, but he could sell the other properties and pay off all the indebtedness if he chose. As it later turned out, Paul was very accurate in believing that our financial situation was much more complicated than Michael had indicated.

Michael said he hated the thought of the children living with me in that house. Paul and Michael's attorney thought that the proposed agreement was more than fair to Michael. Michael and I left the meeting in our separate cars.

LOSING

FRIDAY, MARCH 5: I have a chilling apprehension that some calamitous change is about to happen. I usually try to trust my intuitive hunches, but my life is now so irregular that I don't quite know what to do with this shivery feeling.

I am awed and depressed at the difficulties of living in the same house with an almost-"ex" spouse. The house feels rather like an armed camp, with the two adults alternately avoiding each other, speaking with caution and cold politeness, or bursting into little arguments that feel like tiny firecrackers about to blow the lid off some powder keg. Friends of mine who have come here for the last three weekends, to offer support and help, have unfailingly asked whether I think I am safe living in the same house with Michael right now. He has never been physically violent, but we are also now in a situation that we have never been in before. I respect their intuitions, but Paul advises me to hold on for a few more days until the matter of the agreement is resolved.

Since our second meeting yesterday with our attorneys, Michael has been preoccupied, spooky. The children's lives, and my life as it centers on them, have proceeded pretty much as usual. Alex and Chrissy had a good day at day care today and I brought them back bubbling with stories about snowballs and popcorn. Mary brought home good papers from school and is staying up "as late as I want" because she needn't get up early tomorrow. Jason called from college to say hello and ask how things were proceeding. He said he would be home for the weekend, as was usual for him.

Michael is very quiet. He watches television lying on the couch in the living room, sometimes with Chrissy on his lap, all very much as usual. I am on call at the Emergency Room tonight, and as I come and go through the living room to go out on calls there is a silence, a chill that seems ominous.

Yesterday evening, after that second long negotiating session with the lawyers, Michael asked if I would give him this house. I refused. We both know that we have no immediate resources for me to get other housing here in town for the children and myself. Michael said yesterday to the attorneys and to me that the children didn't care where they lived, and could just as well live in rented rooms for a while. But this house was chosen for them and I hate to disrupt their lives any more than necessary. We have been over and over that issue with the attorneys and I feel that I should follow Paul's advice, that the children and I should stay in this house.

This morning, after the schoolchildren had left and before I took Chrissy to day care, Michael sat down with me at the kitchen table and asked again for a reconciliation. I told him how much I hoped that his life would be better after we parted, how far along I believed that the process of separation had come, how certain I was that it must continue. I felt some vague threat from him at the end of that talk, although I cannot remember his words. All day long I have felt that he is about to do something—something terrible.

After a month of talk about how to work out this divorce, his mood seems to be a mixture of "this isn't really going to happen" and "I must punish her for what she is doing." He seems unaware of the usual legal process. When we talked with the attorneys yesterday he obviously had never even thought about the matter of child-support payments. I think his state now is something like that of a sleepwalker, quite nonrational. I am afraid of what he will do, but I don't know what that is.

The children are my tie to reality and reason. Cooking and

cleaning up for them, sharing meals, washing and ironing their clothes, answering their questions, looking at schoolwork, tucking them in bed and singing lullabies—these familiar chores are my comfort and my assurance that all will be right when this is over. As long as they seem to be doing well, I know that I am functioning adequately for them right now. Guideposts for my own personal well-being are lost for the present.

SATURDAY, MARCH 6: It is almost midnight. I am beginning to know the meaning of that dreadful chill in my bones yesterday.

As I left this morning for my usual Saturday morning office hours, I half heard Michael say to Chrissy that he would take him to buy a new pair of shoes. Michael, Alex, and Christopher were not back for lunch, and then not back for dinner. I have steadfastly done all day what I always do when I have some inkling that my children might be in danger: (1) think whether there is something I can do to safeguard them right now, (2) reassure myself by staying busy with little chores, and (3) deny that any of my horrible fears could be real. When that system of defenses breaks down, I fall into an anxious panic. The panic has come.

Jason, home for the weekend, said that he asked to go along on the shoe-buying trip and was told crossly that only the little boys could go with Michael this time. Jason is also reaching a state of panic as I begin to confront my own fears. Has Michael run away?

Michael's own father, a patient in a psychiatric hospital, escaped from that hospital three times to kidnap his children. Michael always described those episodes with a mixture of rage and pleasure: rage because he, as a small child, had been subject to such uncertainty and loss of control/predictability in his life, and pleasure because of the carnival atmosphere of those runaway trips. Once, I think the last time they were kidnaped, his father threatened to put the three children into an orphanage. The reason for the kidnapings was always that the children's mother was such a "bad" person. They always were rescued in a matter of hours, Michael's mother coming to find them with police sirens screaming and physical battles between the parents, the children literally pulled from one to the other.

Michael speaks with enormous bitterness about his own parents and how damaging their divorce behavior had been for him, his sister, and brother. When we talked to the divorce counselors he talked about not wanting his own children to reenact what he remembers as an angering, helpless situation as a pawn between two embattled adults. When I urged him to help, then, to work out some reasonable terms for our separation he only replied that *I* was setting a train in motion—that whatever happened from my decision onward would be my responsibility, blood on my hands as it were. There was threat in his remarks and an eerie denial of his responsibility. It seemed to me he was saying that if I persisted in my conviction that our marriage must end, then strange and terrible things would happen as an inevitable consequence of my decision.

I went to bed with the doors of the house unlocked, sleeping fitfully. Had he really run away? Perhaps they had only gone for a long drive or to stay overnight in a motel. Michael was always embarking on that sort of spur-of-the-moment trip ("Why shouldn't I take my little boys on a weekend vacation?" was not out of character). Surely, they would come back late in the night or else some time tomorrow. I would have heard if there had been an accident. But I think that I knew then, in my marrow, that this was the start of the train of fright and irrationality that Michael had threatened. Was it really my fault? What had I begun?

I also knew that however Michael might confuse his mother and me, I was not his mother. I was beginning to sense the playing out of Michael's tangle of needs and disappointments: he as his father, with a wife whom he had believed (Michael thought wrongly) to be unfaithful; I as his mother, who never loved him enough nor gave him what he thought he needed and deserved; he as his own child, a helpless victim; and his children as him, getting what he got—whatever the consequences for them—because the father could and must revisit the same pain on his children.

Mary came in to hold me silently before she went to bed. She has a powerful intuitive sense, and I think she knows that there is a hard, worrisome time ahead. Jason is tight-lipped and irritable. I found a scrap of paper that he had doodled on beside the telephone; in one corner, in tiny cramped handwriting, he had written WHERE THE FUCK IS DAD? Tomorrow I must get out of my dream-state of disbelief and talk to each of them.

I wake once in the night—at a strange noise? I check the three empty beds and find them still empty.

SUNDAY, MARCH 7: They are still gone, and the fright unfolds.

Michael's father called at about ten this morning. He is an old man. Michael has had very little communication with him for all the years of our marriage, and usually refers to him as "my poor old father." He asked what was happening "to you folks up there." Ours has been the only enduring marriage among all three of his children, and Michael is the successful child. He sounded confused and sad.

He said that Michael had called him. I don't know the father well enough to be able to tell whether he is lying for Michael or simply telling what happened. I find it impossible to point out to him that Michael is doing just what he himself did. He is obviously calling me on Michael's instructions.

He tells me that Michael wouldn't say where he was but that the operator had a foreign accent. But his real message is that we *must* have a reconciliation. I am stunned and unable to respond to that suggestion. I hear the message that Michael has run away with the little boys and may continue to run, but I am shocked that Michael's intent is to force a *reconciliation*. I don't ask the questions that I should. I feel that his father has become my enemy.

There is nothing that anyone can do right now, at least nothing that I can think of. I am so certain that I must not play out the drama of being Michael's mother, getting the police, trailing him with sirens screaming. Though I still think that to be a possibility (but where would we begin to look?), I consciously choose not to call the police.

All day I hear noises at the front of the house and go to look for Michael's car. At noon we collect for lunch, Jason and Mary and Meg, who has come over because I asked her to. It is Meg who leads me to admit that this is probably not just a weekend excursion. She urges me to go to Michael's office to see if we can discover any clues.

We look on his desk, hoping to find travel-agency messages, and in his checkbook, hoping to find payments for airplane tickets. There is no specific information to be found. But there are bankbooks in several drawers, with varying amounts of money in each—$500 here, $1,400 there—accounts that I didn't know existed. He has cleared out his business account, taken the entire amount as a cash draw. His office is always disordered and there are bits of unfinished business everywhere, including bills, thousands of dollars worth of unpaid bills.

In the middle of the afternoon I begin to understand that others will be affected by his leaving. One of his patients in the hospital has IV fluids running. The nurses are distressed because Michael won't answer his page and they must have a new order for the IV. Will I give the order? Another call comes from another part of the hospital to ask me for advice about a patient who had a heart attack three days ago and now has a fever. Has Michael simply left his patients? I am shocked at such unprofessional behavior and stunned to realize the extent of Michael's irrationality. Will he put Chris and Alex in danger?

Partly in shame and partly from a sense of protectiveness of Michael (how long will I continue to mother him in that way?) I have not wanted to tell anyone in this town that he has gone. Now I call the chief of staff; someone must take responsibility for those patients. He agrees to look in on them and to talk to the nurses about the outstanding orders. He asks if I have spoken with John, the hospital administrator.

When I call John I feel as though I am betraying Michael. John is immediately angry—I am surprised at his controlled fury. He knows more about Michael's unpaid income taxes than I do—apparently a payment of nearly $20,000 was due on March 1. Could this be part of the reason that Michael has run away?

John informs me that I must call the IRS office and talk to Mr. Anderson first thing tomorrow morning. He sounds as if he thinks that I might be colluding in some strange scheme to avoid paying taxes. I tell him of my worry about the children, but he brushes that aside.

Jason and I talk off and on through the day. He is quiet and sad and resentful—I suspect that he is thinking "I have two crazy parents, poor me." Eighteen is a terrible age to be caught in this sort of drama; at that age, one is struggling to attain adult independence. Jason makes a mess everywhere in the house today, and I explode at him in that awful mothering way of making some contact even if it is abrasive and negative. I am struck again, with deep pain, by the realization that I am terribly hard on Jason when he does things that he has learned from observing his father. Worse, sometimes when he does things that might just be characteristic of a teenage son—like neglecting to do chores— I assume that he has learned that from Michael as well. His sullen quiet also reminds me of Michael, and I feel sick that I sometimes see so much of Michael in him. My own grief and preoccupation make it hard for me to give Jason the energy and understanding he needs. I hate myself for having exploded at him so destructively.

All day long I stop and catch my breath in wonder. A reconciliation! We have gone so far with this—can Michael really believe that a reconciliation is still possible? Or that if it were, I could be forced to submit to his will as a response to his running away? When we met with the divorce counselors he said, "I know I can't hold her as my prisoner." Does he not understand that when a relationship has been broken—when trust has been broken—a watershed is passed, a point of no return?

Tomorrow I must try to decide what I can do about all this. I finally reach Paul by telephone tonight and tell him what I think is happening. Paul chills me—he believes that Michael will never come back. Paul has told me before of husbands who were divorced and then simply dropped out of everything that had been familiar and went away to start their lives somewhere else. He thinks Michael is doing that. Unlike John, Paul listens when I tell him of my pain about Alex and Chrissy, my fears for their safety.

I am only beginning to realize what a long stay with Michael will mean for them. No Mommy to put them to bed, to sing favorite lullabies, to answer their endless questions, and to kiss their hurts. And little Alex—his most characteristic pose in Michael's presence is to stand to one side, looking up from under downcast, long-lashed lids, fidgeting with his hands while Michael coddles Chrissy. There is little that Alex can do right for Michael and little that Chris can do wrong. Why did he take Alex with him? Only, I think, because Chrissy loves Alex so and would pine away without him.

I am paralyzed into inaction tonight. I can only wander about the house, picking up and putting down the little boys' books, toys, mittens, pajamas. Michael has taken nothing of their own with them, no familiar reminders of their home and family. Did he not plan to stay away for long? Did he not plan at all? I cannot imagine leaving for even a short trip with a two-year-old and a six-year-old without taking something of their own for them to hold on to.

MONDAY, MARCH 8: I finally reached Susan, Michael's secretary, by telephone. She was not at home all weekend, but in any case she knows little more than I do. Michael called her at home this morning at 6:30 to say that he would "be away indefinitely." She is to advise his patients to see other doctors, but as far as she knows he has not arranged any formal coverage for the patients with whom he has contracted a responsibility. (John was worried, on behalf of the hospital, about inadequate provisions for patients when we talked on the phone yesterday, but I was too anxious about the children to take that in.)

Susan is very restrained with me—polite but distant. She and I used to be comfortable and easy together; she used to call Michael "Dr. Grouch." Does she really believe what Michael has been saying about me, that I am a neglectful mother? I am only beginning to understand that the fact of my employment, and my self-sufficiency, will make me an easy target for rumor and dislike in this town.

A recent influx of fairly prosperous suburbanites is changing the face of this small town near Minneapolis. It is becoming partly a bedroom community; escapees from city life, politically liberal to conservative, are joining with the oldtime residents, who are mostly quite conservative small merchants and farmers, to preserve "this lovely town" from change. There is enough money, in most families, to make the employment of mothers and wives a rarer circumstance than it is in most other cities and towns. By asking Michael for a divorce I probably demonstrated something fearful: a competent, independent woman able to live securely without a man. That upsets the old order that many of them cling to.

I talked to Paul midday. He explained how little there is to do about the runaway. Because divorce papers had not been served we cannot proceed immediately with the divorce; Paul's preoccupation today is the legalistic problem of locating Michael in order to serve papers. Because the divorce proceedings had not come to a point of a temporary hearing, with a custody determination, Michael's snatching of the boys is not illegal; kidnaping laws (for which there are stiff penalties) generally exempt parents, except in some states where it is illegal for the noncustodial parent to kidnap a child. No police system will look for missing persons unless there is some formal, criminal charge. Paul says there is an action called an "attempt to locate" that he will start today through the state police, using the addresses of Michael's relatives and friends that I suggest. But if he is found the police will only notify him that he is to call home. That is not likely to help this situation.

Paul insists that Michael will never come back but reassures me that the boys will be found because a physician is always traceable. He senses my rising panic about their well-being—in the many weeks to come Paul will be one of the very few men who seem to care about the human tragedy of the little boys, or at least about my aching concern for them. He tries to reassure me by proposing that since they are with their father "they must be all right," a remark that I will hear often in the next months and that gives me little comfort, knowing how Michael is with children.

I talk to John again by telephone. He is still very angry at what has happened but says that whatever steps he takes against Michael will have to be considered by the medical staff of the hospital. John will not even hear about the plight of the little boys as a matter of any importance. I realize with a chill that in the "real world" considerations of money and professional responsibility come before the welfare of children. John's anger spills over at me, and once again I feel that he is blaming me for having precipitated something that is causing him, John, a great deal of trouble. John also tells me that Clarence, another doctor in town and the one person Michael might have spoken to in any depth during the past few weeks, has managed to borrow (as of today) enough money for Michael to pay off his overdue tax obligation.

Meg and Barbara and Ann help me to get through a long day of work in the office. I don't believe many people know what has happened—and I feel an odd kind of conspicuous shame (but not, I hope, guilt) that I am caught in this spectacle. I am grateful that I have work to do. It energizes me, turns me away from a sad preoccupation. In niches of time through the day I worry. Are the boys eating well, or mostly candy and junk? Has Alex wet the bed at night and Michael been furious at him? Do they know what is happening to them, what will happen next? Is Alex sad that he is missing school? Will Michael drive safely, watch them as they play near the street? Is he so preoccupied with himself that he cannot take ordinary precautions for them? Is he so caught up in his rage that he is self-destructive, either by direction or by indirection?

Meg and her daughter Molly come to dinner and let me unwind all of the worries and ruminations that I had kept bottled up during my day of work. As we talk I realize that Susan and John and others who don't know me or the story of this marriage might very well blame me for what Michael has done. I now know how important it has been for me to deal with my own ready sense of guilt for the last few weeks. I want to be very clear that what Michael has done is his responsibility. I set nothing into motion except the end of a marriage. Despite my dreads about the consequences of Michael's anger, none of what is now happening could have been foreseen or forestalled. I catch the first taste of my own anger at the assumptions of other people: I was only Michael's wife, not his caretaker, and certainly not his mother. How dare they blame me for what he is doing?

I call Jason at his residence at school. Today he is thoughtful and considerate of me but is keeping himself disengaged from what Michael has done, except for his own grief about the little boys and their safety. I do better at comforting him in our talk today and let his bad temper go by.

I wonder at myself before I go to sleep. My apprehension of responsibility for Michael's actions will die slowly; I have not yet completely taught myself not to feel guilty about what he does. In part he wanted a mother in me and in part I took on that role; our collusion in that was one of the troubles of our marriage. When I agonized fearfully about whether I should insist on a divorce I used to tell myself, "All I have to do is fuck him for sixteen more years, until Christopher is grown enough to be immune from Michael's rages." I am still certain tonight that I could not have done that, nor could I have watched any longer as he made the children feel hopelessly bad, nor could I have allowed him to squander money they would need for education. I had to do what I did. What will the costs be?

TUESDAY, MARCH 9: I call Clarence, timidly, wondering what he thinks he knows about me. As always he talks and talks—whatever he needs to say at the moment. I know well enough from dealing with him before on medical matters that he is not always entirely truthful. He tells me that he is angry with Michael, that he, Clarence, was in a similarly indebted state at the time of his own divorce and that *he* got himself together, paid off his debts, and put his life in order. I hear from him, behind all this tirade, some hint of envy at Michael. Is this the dream of every husband who believes that his wife has forsaken him? Steal her children and run away!

Clarence says that he knows I must be in a terrible state, destroyed, unable to function. He tells me that his first wife once concealed the whereabouts of his own children for several days and he knows how I must feel. Listening to him I am sure that he cannot possibly know how I feel. What man could? I birthed one of those little boys, and I mothered both of them through infancy. I have fed them and bathed them and supervised their hours of day care and weaned them and toilet trained them— *mothered* them. Only another mother could know how much of myself is represented in their welfare. Is it Clarence's projection of himself, or just wishful thinking about the frailties of woman, that makes him tell me that I must be so distraught and incapacitated? I am just beginning to know how deep my reserves of strength really are, just beginning to understand that for the sake of my children and indeed, for the salvation of my own personal integrity, I can be very strong indeed. It looks as if I shall have to be all of that.

Clarence also said that Michael had talked with him about going to Canada, had asked in the doctors' coffee room if it were true that he could avoid responsibility for the IRS debt (and leave it all to me) if he moved to Canada. That news brought me into a momentary flutter of panic that was to become very familiar to me in the next several weeks. Could they be traced, if they were in Canada?

When I talked to Susan later in the day she asked if I knew that Michael had gotten a check from the hospital on Friday, the day before he left. Someone had called her from the hospital business office and said "his check is ready." Susan remembered that she was surprised because she usually conducted all of Michael's business with hospital offices. She had asked him if he wanted her to go pick up the check and he had said, "No, no, I'll get it myself," which was so unusual that it made her wonder.

I left my office immediately after I heard that news and went to the hospital to talk to John. He wasn't there, and his secretary seemed less than candid in response to my questions. The hospital business manager stopped in and she told him, "Michael's wife knows about that check." The looks they exchanged implied that the topic was troublesome. Just then John came back to his office.

John said, "Michael called me at home last night."

I said, "For God's sake, John, what kind of a game are you playing with me? Why didn't you tell me?"

He said, "Michael says you have to get out of that house. He is charging that because of your feminism you are a neglectful mother." John searched my face with a faint, smug grin.

I sighed. "John, that's nonsense. How much money did you give him on Friday?"

"How did you find out about that? Michael asked me for four thousand dollars more—and you know that five months ago his earnings put him beyond the limits of the guarantee. But he said that he needed the money for household expenses, and especially to pay your son's college tuition. I gave him a check for two thousand dollars. He tricked me—that must be the money he's running away with. He got that under false pretenses."

Paul called later in the day to say that there were no balances in any of Michael's bank accounts. We reconstructed some four or five thousand dollars that Michael had gotten together on Friday, just out of those several accounts. I began to wonder about all the money we never seemed to have over those years. Had Michael always squirreled away sums for his own use? Why, indeed, did we always seem so poor in pocket money and why did Michael always believe that he could afford to buy anything he wanted?

When the mail came at my office this afternoon there was a misdelivered package addressed to Michael—two hundred and fifty dollars' worth of very expensive shirts, bought the day that Michael went to consult an out-of-state attorney. Michael's tranquilizer—making expensive purchases. I have just discovered that there are about three thousand dollars' worth of unpaid household-expense bills lying in the clutter of Michael's desk at home. Meg reassured me about those: by state law Michael is responsible for household expenses until we are finally divorced. Still, I was horrified and ashamed, I who never let bills go unpaid for more than a week or so.

I have very little money. Paul says that I should not pay on any of Michael's obligations, at least not yet. We reviewed the situation on the three pieces of property and agreed that there would have to be some way to cover the payments on the three mortgages. I called Michael's tenants in the house we used to live in in Chicago and heard a stream of puzzled complaints about his chronic inaccessibility and their relief at hearing from me. Yes, of course, they would send the rent check in my name—and they were sorry to hear about the trouble. But they didn't exactly sound surprised. I am beginning to understand how much I have covered over and compensated for Michael's behavior, both publicly and privately, and how odd and arrogant and unreasonable he seems to many people.

Jason called me. He had called at Michael's father's house and had been told by the old man that he didn't know where Michael was. Jason said he left the message that he loved Michael and that he must bring the little boys back home. I had been unwilling to give the father's telephone number to anyone, in the first forty-eight hours after Michael left, but today I gave the number to Paul, to pass along to Michael's attorney, and to John as well.

At supper time I got a call from Michael's brother—three times married, three times divorced, a man who enjoys woman-hating talk. He scolded me about resisting a reconciliation. He also said, "Tell your friends not to call my father—he has a bad heart." I felt guilty about the old father, until I remembered who had made those calls—Michael's own son, his boss (in a sense) at the hospital, and his own attorney. The family members who were answering the telephone could screen those calls for the old man if they wished.

Jason called back at midnight. He had just had a call from Michael. He thought that Michael's message was directed to me—the first of a long series of telephone calls and letters apparently addressed to others but in fact primarily meant for me. He had, he said, everything that he cared about in the trunk of his car: his medical licenses, his diplomas, the children's birth certificates, everything. And he had plenty of money. He intended to stay gone for as long as he "had to," forever if necessary. Jason asked how he would know that he didn't have to stay away anymore. Michael said, "When your mother decides to do things my way— she knows what I mean." Jason said that Michael would not listen to any reasoned discussion, so that Jason finally said that he loved Michael and that he hoped he would bring Alex and Chrissy home soon.

What does he mean, do things his way? Paul and I have talked about this. Paul believes that there should be no bargaining with Michael now, that his blackmail-demands would be insatiable if we started that. Is it still reconciliation that he is asking for? What if I collapsed in a heap of quivering anxiety, went raving mad, moved away from this town, told Michael that I couldn't survive without him? What would satisfy him now?

Could I, in fact, promise a reconciliation that I was not willing to go through with? That is what some of my friends have suggested, and I find the idea repellent, not only because there is no way that I could ever be his wife again but even more because that seems to require a despicable degree of dishonesty. I am not a good actress, and despite nineteen years of pretending that our marriage was going along all right I do not think that I could carry off that conversation convincingly. If I did, I would have been knowingly and intentionally dishonest with Michael in a way that I never had been before. It seemed to me that if I tricked him in that way he would have a real reason to hate me, to pursue me vengefully and forever. My deepest fear, over and above the very present worry about the safety of my children, is that Michael would find ways to continue to involve himself in my life even after the divorce was over. No, I could not promise or even hint at a reconciliation, not even to rescue Chris and Alex, at least not until I had exhausted all other avenues.

I am burning vigil candles.

WEDNESDAY, MARCH 10: A day of discouragements. A father has a right to kidnap his children, apparently. Unless he has committed a crime (apart from this kidnaping) there is no way to stop him.

There is some considerable sympathy for what Michael has done. Clarence told me yesterday that Michael told many people —nurses, lunch-table companions, his patients—that I was a neglectful mother. Some of those people believe that he has done a good and noble thing to leave his busy practice to "rescue" those poor neglected children from my hands. That makes me speechless with frustration and fury.

I called all three of the credit companies for which Michael has credit cards. In two of the calls, when I told the rather distant and businesslike men that Michael had run away, left his patients, kidnaped two small children, had no current source of income, and was likely to use his credit cards to charge the expenses of his runaway, they each remarked, "It sounds like a marital dispute to me, lady, and we can't get involved." In the third call I spoke to a woman who was horrified at the story and said she thought they could cancel his card and would let me know where he was the next time he tried to charge on the card. By the end of the conversation she sounded a little doubtful. Perhaps, she said, they could not legally take any steps.

I have also learned that it is not possible to put a tap on my telephone so that we could locate him if he ever called. One can only tap a private phone for obscene calls, and nothing that a husband might say to a wife would ever count as obscene—rather like the ruling that a husband can never be charged with raping his wife.

Michael was reported in the "attempt to locate" to be at his father's house this morning. Paul has sent a set of divorce papers to the sheriff there, to serve him if he has not already left. I feel certain that he will have left there, now that he knows he has been located.

I find myself in the very difficult position of being the only person (except Jason to a lesser degree) who knows Michael well. He has no close friends. The only people who have any suggestions that seem to me to be useful are those friends of mine who are or have been married to angry, suspicious, childish men. I have to convince Paul and John and even Clarence that I know there are some things Michael will not do and some things he is likely to do.

Paul talked to a lieutenant in the state police today and confirmed what we already thought we knew: they will make no effort to find Michael, nor to retrieve the little boys, unless a criminal charge is filed for some offense other than stealing children.

The situation with the money and property is equally mind-boggling. Our two pieces of out-of-state property are jointly owned but I cannot sell them to pay debts unless Michael signs over the deeds to me. I am obligated for the tremendous expenditures of the monthly mortgage payments just to hold steady in a position of terrible indebtedness.

All those years as his wife, blindly signing for debts and responsibilities in the face of "what's the matter, don't you trust me?" If I had said I didn't trust him—even if I had only asked to keep my financial affairs separate from his—I would have violated the sense of our original contract and he would have made my life as his wife harder than it was. As long as I believed that it was worthwhile to try to sustain that marriage, I was trapped into allowing him to manage our finances.

The saddest jest of all is that his legal right of access to the children comes only from his obligation to support me and the children. I never needed him to support us. Why *did* I think I needed a husband nineteen years ago? It seems to me now that my perception of that need had primarily to do with a sense of proportion—I was brought up to believe that a family must have a certain configuration, a mother, a father, and children. The law has always said, in various degrees and shades, that the father/husband holds his place and rights basically by virtue of his financial support. Knowing as I did that I would be able by my own work to support myself and even to support children, I opted for a marriage of companionship and some sharing in the running of a household. The companionship was more destructive than rewarding and the hope of sharing was a cause for endless battles.

Now I am the subject of severe criticism—from John, Paul, the IRS, and from myself as well—for having been so stupid as to have signed my name to indebtedness that I didn't even know the extent of. This is surely a double trap for women, especially those who are self-supporting. If I were young and starting a marriage again I would insist that all our property ownership, indebtedness, and bill paying be individual. I would also want a contract agreed upon before marriage that clarified the separation of property in the event of dissolution of the marriage.

I used to think that there was something crass and commercial and not very human about the linkage of child-support payments by separated fathers with their rights of visitation. Now I am inclined to believe that I respect that connection: it lays bare the convention by which our legal and social systems operate, that fathers have a right to contact with their children as a consequence of their obligation to support. That is the root of the father-right, which exists over and above any tie of affection, caring, or knowledge about the well-being of the child. Paul and others have said time and time again that courts rarely deny the right of a father to have access to his children, no matter what kind of a person he is nor how destructive to a child. The mother-right, on the other hand, comes out of the obligation to take care of and *can* be challenged on the basis of an examination of the quality of care. In some cases mother-right has been denied on the grounds that the mother is employed, possibly self-supporting, and not devoting her full time to child care. Here is what I, as a woman and a mother, have learned this week. *It can be very dangerous to let anyone have legal rights to your children.*

THURSDAY, MARCH 11: Meg, Barbara, Ann, and I talked in the office today about the rumors that patients report to us, primarily rumors that I am a neglectful mother. Our patients are supportive, but it is clear that Michael asked for and found a great deal of sympathy, before he ran away, and that much of that sympathy was gained at my expense. I am overwhelmed with anger and sadness at the loss of trust between Michael and me and at my innocence about his vindictiveness. While I was working to give him time and space to come to an understanding about the end of our marriage, he was slandering me in every way he could imagine. Is this all an effort to try to take the children away from me in a court battle?

Those fragile threads of attachment between Michael and me, which I valued as a residue of nineteen years of marriage, are being wantonly torn apart by him when I had hoped to cherish and strengthen them. Perhaps Michael feels that if he can't have me as his wife then he must work to discredit and destroy me in every way he can imagine. I would have liked for the children and me to have some continuing contact with him, but I am beginning to wonder whether there will be any basis for that contact.

I have gone through these past few days in the belief that Alex and Chrissy will be back with me soon, any day now. I cannot quite envision how that might happen, but I want to believe that Michael will come to his senses and simply drive back into town. But I am beginning to hear stories that frighten me deeply, about children lost for months or even years. This sort of parental kidnaping is not infrequent, apparently. More and more often, in recent years, the kidnapers have been fathers. What I think I am hearing about is an increase in the number of angry husbands who have chosen this means to punish their wives. The people I have talked to about these cases say that the children themselves are secondary in the meaning of the act. The real issue is the punishment of the mother.

I heard a song today that I have listened to many times without hearing the words. Hearing it today was like a knife stab. The refrain goes, "Child of my body, bone of my bone, apple of my eye." I feel that no one really understands the pain I carry inside—except, perhaps, another mother who has endured something like this. I wonder and I worry about my children. I feel as if a piece of me is missing. When Jason left, grown, to go away to school it was as if a piece of me dried up, became scar tissue. I can still press that mother-scar and feel a tingling, a reminiscence of all those years of my caring for him in the mother/child way. But for Alex and Chrissy it is as if two mothering pieces of me have been torn away—by a vulture or a monster—too soon, prematurely, long before they were ready to shrink and dry up and become strong, healed places for me. It feels as if two lactating, full, overflowing breasts were torn out of me, leaving raw wounds and reaching-out pain. I am only beginning to understand what it means for a mother to lose a child.

I have not cried. I know I will soon, whenever the time comes. I have talked with many friends, some whom I have called and some who have called me after hearing the news from the network of good and caring women I know as friends. Two calls, both long distance, were purely intuitive—friends who had hunches that they should call and ask if everything were all right.

I keep very busy. Mary seems relatively at peace, although she cried again last night when she went to bed. Between tending to her and to my work, keeping the household running, talking to friends, and conferring with Paul about what can be done, there are hardly any chinks left in my day. I don't want those chinks right now—I want to dull the pain.

FRIDAY, MARCH 12: Michael called me this morning. He sounded distraught, tense, angry, ill. He wouldn't say where he was, said that he would never tell me that. I asked to talk to Christopher and Alex and he refused.

I said, "Michael, they have to be able to talk with the people here who love them and whom they love."

He said, "They are with the people who love them."

He said he would never come back. He must have rehearsed what he would say, for it came out in tight little rushes. I begged him to consider his career as a physician. He said, "I can earn enough to support my little boys by being a ditchdigger or a hospital orderly."

He called me a "greedy bitch," said it was well known that divorce courts were always unfair to men, and he felt that he had to take matters into his own hands to "force the issues." While we talked I felt tightly calm, as if I were talking to someone at the window of a high building who was threatening to jump, trying to think of reasons for him to care about his future, trying to say what I had to say in words that would be soothing and not inflaming. I said that everything we had talked about could be renegotiated.

He said repeatedly that this was all my fault, that I was making this happen—I should have thought of this before I said I wanted a divorce. The tension of his voice and the staccato effect of his words made me heartsick for Alex and Chrissy. The distraction of Michael's rage must be terrifying for them. Probably they sense his need and are taking care of him, as children do.

Tonight for the first time I cry and cry and cry. A friend calls and I have to tell her that I cannot talk. I know that I worry her, but I cannot pull myself together even to speak one coherent sentence.

It feels as if this evil might endure, might overcome all the good forces that I believe have bathed me. I grew up wanting to trust that if one were good and caring and tried to do right then things would come out all right. I never realized before tonight how much I had wanted to believe in that system of rewards, that universe of proportion and grace. And yet, here is Michael doing this awful thing, hurting not just himself but also and especially the children in his effort to hurt me. I am so afraid that harm, both physical and psychological, will come to Alexy and Chrissy, my babies. I look tonight at my own pain, straight on. I feel as if I hate Michael.

SEARCHING

WEDNESDAY, MARCH 17: I mother Mary, see my patients and do my ordinary work, and run the household—and every day is filled with the search for Chris and Alex. I start each day with a long list of ideas of new ways to push and probe, trying to get some help in the search. As long as I feel there is something I can do— even if most of my efforts come to nothing—I can hold myself together.

I am astounded with the good fortune of having Paul to help me in this. He is chagrined by his decision not to serve papers before Michael ran away. More than that, I think he worries about the boys, or at least he responds to my very obvious distress. In this Paul differs from almost everyone I talk to, except of course the women who are my friends. It seems as if for most people the boys are objects in a contest, not defenseless little people at risk of great harm.

Michael telephoned again on Sunday. He asked to and did speak to Jason and Mary. (He sent letters that arrived yesterday to both of them, telling them what a good "vacation" trip he and Alex and Chris were on. Mary read her letter in silence, then tore it up.) I asked that we be able to speak to the little boys and he let us. Jason and Mary and I each told them that we missed them, that their friends missed them, that their puppy missed them, that we all loved them, and they should come home very soon. They are too little to be very talkative on the telephone; they said that

Daddy said they couldn't come home, and that they were playing with guns.

One of our very unpleasant disagreements about child rearing happened last year. I have always urged that the children not be supplied with toy guns and be gently discouraged from using sticks in shoot-'em-up play. Michael spends a great deal of time in the evenings watching television and often insisted on keeping Chrissy up very late in the evening so that Chrissy also saw much violence on TV just before he fell asleep. As a consequence, Chrissy's talk and play were full of violence and gun play—killing people, smashing them, crashing cars, and fights to the death. Despite my pleas, Michael was unwilling to give up either his television-watching habits or Chrissy's bedtime arrangements. And now they *are* playing with guns and telling me about it defiantly.

In his conversation with me, the reason for his telephone call, Michael repeatedly said that I was a neglectful mother because I cared more about my work than about my family. Always, since he first met me, I have been a full-time student or worker, and always he has been proud of that. At the same time he has been openly proud of my mothering care of the children. Now it is as if he believes that I worked outside of the house only with his permission, and with his permission withdrawn I become the employed mother who risks harm to her children by her employment. Michael knows as well as I that there is no factual basis for that accusation about employed mothers. Often, in research studies, their relationship with their children is found to be better than that of full-time-housewife mothers. But there are plenty of tradition-minded people out there who will listen to him and agree if he claims that I have been selfish and neglectful of the children because I have also occupied myself with interesting work.

He then accused me of greed for expecting him to pay some child-support money, on the general grounds that mothers who are employed do not "deserve" child support. (This feels like a classic Catch 22.) I have never demanded child-support money, but Paul has warned me that I can't give that right away (even to lure Michael back with the children). Our state law requires that some support be awarded. Of course child-support awards are often not honored. If I remember the research, about two-thirds of fathers fail to comply in full with child-support orders in the first year after the court order, many do not make even a single payment, and after ten years most are paying nothing of the ordered amounts. Divorced mothers usually get poorer, while divorced fathers more often increase their own available income. I simply told Michael that paying child support was a matter for him and his conscience.

A letter came from him today. It was postmarked Cleveland. Michael had boasted to Jason when he last called him at school that he had a secret way of posting letters. A friend, another cardiologist, was acting as intermediary. He was posting Michael's mail from Cleveland.

Anna:

I am "Head of Household" for our family. I have decided to move our residence. Until I find a permanent location, our family's new address is:

[he has given his father's address]

For the time being—since I am not now at work—I expect you will not have enough money to live on. My father can help, if you find yourself in difficulty—just send Mary to him and he will provide her support.

Concerning my own belongings: Jason may have any or all of my clothes —I expect he would enjoy wearing them. Everything else you may dispose of as you wish. I care not at all about any of it.

Sincerely,

For all of my anger at him and my own pain, I cannot help but grieve for his obvious unhappiness. He is reacting to a situation already painful—the divorce—by causing more pain for everyone, himself included. I can understand that he might need to run away, agonize, be crazy for a while. But he has no right or reason to take two defenseless children with him.

I have talked with John about the hospital's part in this almost every day for the past week. Paul says that if the hospital would get involved, and if extradition could be arranged, that would be the best chance of getting the boys back. Michael and his automobile would be called to the attention of all state police and he would eventually be picked up (perhaps for something like a speeding violation, perhaps just because his car is noticed as an out-of-state car). Certainly he cannot be allowed to continue to flee with those two little boys, and it does not seem that he will listen to any kind of reason.

I now think John should encourage the hospital to become involved—but he is reluctant to do so. There is no question, apparently, that the money was obtained under false pretenses. But John is not so sure that the managing board of the hospital will agree to get involved. They believe, says John, that the whole affair is essentially a family dispute.

I feel very bad about all this. I wish the hospital would do whatever it can to get Michael—or rather, the boys—back. I am angered at the attitude, "It's a family dispute and we don't want to get involved," angered that Michael can receive that kind of backhanded support for what he is doing, and angered that small children don't count in the world of grown-up men.

John tosses off my worries about Alex and Chris. He tells me what others also say—"Since we know that Michael is fond of the little boys they must be all right." I do know that they are not likely to come to any physical danger with him, unless of course he is so distraught that he just fails to take ordinary precautions against all the dangers that this world offers to little children. But the combination of Michael's ordinary insensitivity to children and his present state of fury/grief/disorganization must be frightening and confusing, if not actually abusive, for them.

I worry especially about Alex, for Michael has very little empathy with that child. I remember the teachers at Alex's day-care center calling me in, time and time again, to worry about the way Michael treated Alex when he picked him up at the end of the day. They were shocked and dismayed at the abusiveness of his words and his tone of voice. I would reassure them—protecting Michael, again—by saying that he got very angry with the children but he was also very loving, and they were used to him. It

was like being in that public restaurant again. I finally arranged
to do both the bringing to and the picking up at the day-care
center. That, however, only served to hide Michael's abuse of
Alex from outsiders' eyes and didn't change the way he treated
him in private.

Some things are becoming very clear to me. It is a degrading
thought that any parent has a "right" to a child—in the words of
a legal phrase that I read recently, "a natural inclination to *possess* the object of his affection" (italics mine). What right could
one have to another person?

We have obligations to each other, responsibilities, ties, loyal-
ties, attachments. We earn each other's welcome by our trust-
worthiness or beauty or service or nurturance. But we cannot
have rights to another.

But it could be argued that children are different. They cannot
care for themselves; they must be taken care of. The responsibility
of taking care of a sometimes crying, unreasonable, runny-nosed,
demanding, thankless brat is not always joyous. Perhaps it is assumed, then, that there must be, as reward, some *right* to balance
that *responsibility*. Therein lies precisely the point of the dilemma
of parenting on which mothers have been impaling themselves
forever. For despite the responsibility and the obligation there can
be no right to the child. There can only be the myriad of small
pleasures of loving and caring, the attachment that grows out of
the investment of time and energy and self, and the wonder at
growth, change, becoming. The mothering obligation is to finish
what began in the womb.

The father-right ("no judge will ever deny a father access to his
child") is based on the father's obligation to support his child
financially, according to our social and legal customs. The mother-
right is in fact *only* obligation, not to the child but to the fathers:
to the one support-providing father, who is usually the biological
father, and to those others who will use our children as workers,
soldiers, students, readers, voters, statistics, after we have delivered
them to adulthood.

If we accorded children the same full personhood that we pretend to accord to all adults equally, we would know that parents,

mothers and fathers, can only earn their children's welcome. Feeding, bathing, stroking, responding, bandaging, soothing, limiting, expanding—in short, all of the efforts of caring for—are the coins through which we earn that welcome. That earned welcome, which we sometimes call attachment, is not a prerogative of mothers only. But mothers have a head start, having borne and birthed and (sometimes) nursed. In addition, in this society, mothers have also been forced (some willingly, some not) to be primary and primarily child-caretakers while men have had "important" things to do.

There are, then, relationships of ownership between parents and children. Fathers are assumed to have rights of access to their children, exactly as if they were pieces of property, without any examination of the quality of the relationship. Mothers have primarily *relationship* rights of access to children. Examination of the nature of a mother's relationship can produce grounds for taking children away from mothers, but mothers do not have the same kind of legal property rights that fathers do. Children themselves do not even have the legal protections that hold for actual property. If Michael had stolen a painting of the two boys we could probably find him and force him to return the painting, especially if it had a known and significant monetary value.

The other side of what I am learning out of this legal tangle is that a man is presumed to have a right to do (almost) anything he wishes to a wife, rather in the manner that parents used to be free to punish their children in their own homes and in the interests of discipline, however harsh that punishment might be. In some places the law used to say that even if a parent killed a child as a result of punishment, that was not an act to be criminally prosecuted because that was private parental behavior and not subject to public review.

I think that the same attitude exists today with respect to public review of extreme actions on the part of husbands against wives. (It may be argued that there is an equal reluctance to interfere with the actions of wives against husbands, but both public sympathy and the preponderance of strength and will to hurt are tilted on the side of husbands.) In the minds of many of the men I have talked to, our present situation represents Michael's effort to punish me for saying that I no longer want to live with him. They are comfortable and feel justified in recommending that the matter be allowed to work itself out without outside interference. "Sounds like a marital dispute to me, lady." I have learned to ask for information and help with respect to the kidnaping without volunteering that Michael's actions are in part a response to my request for a divorce. His actions are also, I am sure, a response to his acute money crisis, and for most people *that* is readily understood as a reprehensible situation made worse by running away.

I had a talk with two of the Emergency Room nurses today—a tearful talk, on my part. The constant dribble of rumors in the town that I was a neglectful mother seems to originate from hospital personnel, who have their information directly from Michael. How can I defend myself against that charge of neglect? How can I prove that I bake almost all our household bread, that I have taught the older children how to cook, that I sing lots of lullabies and game songs with them, that I have always known the children's teachers very well and been in close touch with them, that I have read their children's books to them so many times that I know them by heart? What *is* a good mother, anyway? How can I convince anyone who has not come to our house that I am attentive and caring, that the children *come* to me (as they never do to Michael) for approval and affection and attention? All that the nurses could say, probably to comfort me in my obvious distress, was that they liked to work with me, that they respected my care of patients and my cooperation with hospital staff. I still don't know who in the hospital is pushing these rumors, nor how to stop them. Apparently Michael is continuing to call people here in town, trying to keep the whole messy scandal alive.

FRIDAY, MARCH 26: The hospital has hired an attorney, Oscar Larson, to represent them in any action against Michael. Paul believes that they will never get involved. They assume that if they simply wait for Michael and not move against him he will finally repay the money he owes them. At this point I do not care whether the hospital is repaid or not. I only care that the children are found. Paul keeps reminding me that the two issues are entirely separate—that for the hospital only the money is of concern and the fate of the children is irrelevant. In fact, it is increasingly clear that no agency that can act to find Michael has any interest in the well-being of the children.

I keep saying, in despair, "No one will help!" Meg scolds me— I must have had more than fifty phone calls from people who have heard the story and want to do something to help. Some have given real help: Nancy arranged to sell second-hand equipment for me so that I can pay some of the outstanding household bills, and Dianne sent $25 as "a stone for stone soup," a seed for other kinds of help. But the frightening and frustrating thing for all of us is that I don't know what to tell my friends to do. I don't know where to start.

Paul has been working on the possibility of getting the FBI involved, since they have a better search-and-find network than any other agency. There is a bill in Congress now that would overturn the present exemption of parents from the federal kidnaping statute. An organization called Children's Rights, Inc., which is made up of parents whose children have been kidnaped by the other parent, is serving as a lobbying group for that bill. If the bill were passed, kidnaping by a noncustodial parent would be dealt with like other kinds of kidnaping and the FBI would have to look for stolen children. The FBI and the Justice Department are lobbying vigorously against this legislation on the grounds that "the federal government can't do everything," "there are too many cases of child stealing that would require FBI work," and "the FBI shouldn't be getting involved with marital disputes." So for now, and unless that bill is passed, there is no nationally coordinated (and uniform-across-states) public policy with regard to the fate of children stolen by a parent.

Paul has another possible avenue of approach to federal assistance. The money owed to the Internal Revenue Service—which Michael did not even tell me about until the week before he ran away—is my debt as well as his, since I (trustingly) signed a joint tax return. Michael acknowledged very publicly, just before he left, that that debt was morally his because my share of the tax was paid out of my salary deduction and because he had failed to inform me of his failure to pay his owed tax. Paul has been trying to get the IRS to look for Michael, at least to take his car, to pay on that debt. But the IRS agents know from Michael that we own property jointly, and they are only interested in getting their money as simply as possible. They have already attached our vacation cabin and land and will sell it in a "tax sale." It will probably be sold for much less than it is worth, as is usually the case in such a sale, and the asset will be lost. At least that sale would relieve the pressure on me of the tax debt, since the property is worth far more than the amount of the debt. Paul will continue to urge the IRS to look for Michael, but I am not hopeful that that avenue will be of any use to us.

There are also two possible federal offenses for which FBI help might be sought. One is Michael's receipt of $2,000 from the hospital. A friend in Washington has suggested that if fraud was involved and if the money originally came from Medicaid-Medicare, the FBI would want to know about it.

The other long shot involves a letter that Michael wrote to a bank at the time that our present house was bought, a letter promising that the proceeds from the sale of our former home would be applied toward a loan that Michael was taking and that I also cosigned. I suspected at the time what has since become clear, that Michael had no intention of selling that other house. That letter may be technically fraudulent and, since the bank is a federal reserve bank, that may also be a reason for the FBI to become involved.

Paul is discussing both of these matters with the chief FBI agent for the state. He is an approachable man and has told Paul that he would be glad to do whatever he can but only if there is some good indication that a federal statute has been violated. I vacillate between hope that we will get help (from any source) and a dread sick feeling that they will stay gone, and stay gone forever—with God knows what kind of damage to Alexy and Chrissy. What a lot of complicated, far-reaching red tape to sort through to find a reason to look for two small boys!

I have thought about child-abuse resources. I have not yet approached that route—I don't even know how to begin. I will start that tomorrow.

This preoccupation is incredibly time-consuming. I spend hours on the telephone—every night I make the list of ten or twenty things I must do the next day on behalf of the boys. My telephone bill is gigantic. I have very little money saved—all of it will go toward finding the boys, if that is necessary. Meg is right—my worst days are the days when I cannot think of any action to take. That is true even when I admit that most of the routes of help I have investigated come to naught and might be counted by someone else as "wasted" time, effort, and expense. I will not, cannot rest until the boys are back. I must try every avenue, every means to find them and bring them back. I am best comforted, can best control the weight of my worry and grief when I can convince myself that I am not helpless, that there is something I can do about the boys' welfare and my pain. I am devastated when I feel we are trapped, at Michael's mercy, and shouldered away by every agency that is supposed to defend the troubled and the oppressed, the victims of wrongdoing. I am especially devastated when I confront my own personal sense of loss and powerlessness.

Mary's birthday is next week. Jason and Mary and I each wrote letters last week to Alex and Christopher, sending them to Michael's father to be forwarded. I don't have much hope that the letters will actually be read to them, but I do feel that we must do whatever we can to reassure them that their ordinary world still exists, waits for them, wants them back. Mary added a postscript, addressed to Michael, in her letter: "Please come home for my birthday. They say at school that you will never come back. I do not want to believe that."

There was another phone call from Michael to the house tonight. He called primarily to assure Jason that he would pay his tuition next year. Michael wouldn't let any of us talk to the boys and screamed his usual accusatory abuse at me. He told Jason, "I put my life in your mother's hands nineteen years ago, and she has betrayed me." Even eighteen-year-old Jason finds that a frightening basis for a marriage between adults.

Has Michael always thought of me, or felt toward me, as the mother he wanted as a child, believed he deserved and never had, a mothering-person now possessed, purchased (through the obligation to support), and therefore able to control? Certainly I have sometimes played a mothering role with him. There are so few models for adult women to relate to men, and we do tend to fall back on those stereotypic familial roles of daughter and mother. I am willing to believe that Michael and I both contributed to that aspect of our relationship. While it was going on I thought it not entirely unreasonable, since it "worked" to keep us together. But now, in the struggle of separation, I find it sickly and sickening.

Now I have turned my back on Michael (something that his mother could never do—she just kept pushing him away until *he* turned his back on *her*) and I become all of the things that he hated in his mother. Maybe I am learning a lesson: never marry a man who says he hates his mother. His talk on the telephone to me now is *woman*-hating, and perhaps the genesis is *mother*-hating. Do all men who are dissatisfied with their own mothers become mother-fuckers? Can mothers ever fulfill for their children what this society dictates that we should be and do? Am I rearing my own sons to feel chronically deprived of eternal, unflagging, unselfish, sacrificing, and endlessly giving mother-love, so that they too will want when they are grown to buy women who will satisfy their mothering needs on demand?

We mothers certainly contribute to that dilemma if we follow the dictates of society and push our little boys away, deny them nurturing, tell them they must be brave and mustn't cry, must act like "little men." We are told that we should represent ourselves to them as able to interpret their emotions for them, as endlessly capable of comforting and coddling. But also, we are told to tell them they can't have that part of us lest they turn into sissies. We only send them on to search for more and better mothering, this time by an owned piece of property that will not be allowed to defect or withdraw or refuse, a piece of property that can be coerced to continue and punished for leaving. The coercions and the punishments are so structured into society that it would take an unusual man to resist them as they are offered through the legal system and in the conventional opinions of the social world.

THURSDAY, APRIL 1: Michael did not come back for Mary's birthday. She seems to want to put him out of her mind. I think that in her careful, precise, testing way she told herself that if he didn't respond to her request to return himself and Alex and Chris for her birthday, she would give up on him. She came crying to me again last night at bedtime—she had had a difficult day in school, couldn't understand her arithmetic homework, and had been working on it at home. She said, "I can't concentrate on my work with the boys gone—I miss them so very much," and burst into tears. What a lot of rents in our lives there will be to mend after this is over!

It will surely be all over one day—I must constantly reassure myself of that, even at the moments that it seems as if it could go on forever. Every few days I stop myself, try to take stock of the larger picture. I could probably just go on with my life if I knew that my two little sons were dead, or even that I would never ever see them again—as Michael threatened in his last phone call. I would know that we who remained constituted our family and could properly grieve for their loss. But I can't do that, can't stop trying to find the boys and bring them back, as long as I know there is any hope of succeeding in that. I begin to understand the pain of families whose loved ones are reported missing in action.

That last phone call came at 2:30 A.M. The phone started ringing at 8:00 in the evening and I didn't answer it, thinking that it was probably he and not feeling I had the strength to listen to another tirade of abuse. It is my intuition that it is important for me not to lash out at him when he is so abusive, thinking that he must be soothed into rationality. One aspect of my sense of helplessness is that he can call us but we cannot contact him— that makes me feel like a butterfly impaled on a pin, unable to fight off the ripping of my wings. And since I keep hoping that one day Michael will call and there will be some important information I must know—they are coming back, or one of the boys is hurt or sick—I have not been able to resist answering the phone and listening to him. But last night I hadn't the strength for that, recognizing how overcome with anger and helpless sadness I was after every call.

The phone rang every hour through the evening. Finally, at 2:30, when I was awakened out of a deep sleep, I counted twenty rings and suddenly panicked that one of the boys was sick or injured. When I answered Michael plunged into his abuse. He said he would never pay on the delinquent household bills, they would stop bringing us milk and oil, we would freeze and starve. "And you can shove that up your frigid fanny." I hung up.

Ellen, my old friend and co-worker, is here to visit for a few days. She said to me, as we were washing up the dinner dishes, "For all of your grief, I can't tell you how glad I am that you finally decided to divorce him. You know, you are very good at putting firm fences around the things you are willing to talk about. I never felt that I could talk with you about Michael. Do you know I have felt physically sick when I was in your house and heard the way he talked to the children?"

I felt still a little shy about explaining away that time of my life. I said, "No, I didn't know that about you, but I have heard from other friends that they felt the same way. Pat said that she simply wouldn't come to the house when he was at home. You know, I always felt that it would be an unforgivable violation of my contract with him to talk about our difficulties with anyone else."

Ellen smiled that brilliant, soft smile of hers. "Yes, but you do know that that is the classic wife's trap. As long as you must publicly cover over and conceal the difficulties, you cannot get the strength to break away. You did talk to me a little, twice—do you remember? The first time was after I spoke to you about Michael's conversation with me when he said that he beat the children fairly severely but he didn't think it really hurt them. I told him I had been beaten as a child and I knew it hurt. You said then that you were determined to stay with it, to make it work. You thought the good outweighed the bad."

I said, wiping the counters with savage energy, "There is a funny kind of reverse-coin phenomenon connected with that. As long as I felt I had to stay in the marriage, the positives *had* to outweigh the negatives. As soon as I decided I could not stay, then the values changed and the negatives outweighed the positives."

Ellen put her arm around my shoulder. "The other time we talked I understood much more about that. You said Michael had no friends, that you were his only friend. You said, 'what would he do without me?' Of course what he is doing now proves you were right, but you must know that it cannot be your responsibility to save his soul, at your expense and at the expense of the children. At least that talk helped me to understand why you had let all of this go on for so long."

John, the hospital board, and Oscar Larson are still saying that if they have to wait much longer for Michael to return they will have to get involved. But I don't think anyone is telling Michael that, and the threat value of that plan is probably its greatest advantage. For my own self-interest, I don't want to see Michael hurt. I hope he can come out of this as healthy and functioning as possible.

At John's urging I spoke to the hospital board. They are nine solemn men of late middle age, pillars of this community. Clearly, they saw me as "wife" and not at all as "physician." I could not beg from them for the sake of my children—I did not think they would understand. I thought of part of Susan Griffin's poem,

> . . . sometimes
> I think of the President
> and other men,
> men who practice the law,
> who revere the law,
> who make the law,
> who enforce the law
> who live behind
> and operate through
> and feed themselves
> at the expense of

starving children
because of the law,
men who sit in paneled offices
and think about vacations
and tell women
whose care it is
to feed children
not to be hysterical
not to be hysterical as in the word
hysterikos, the greek for
womb suffering,
not to suffer in their
wombs,
not to care,
not to bother the men
because they want to think
of other things
and do not want
to take the women seriously.
I want them
to take women seriously.

I am sorry now that I ever went to their meeting.

I have looked into the possibility of a child-abuse charge. As a physician I know I am obligated to be concerned about and to call to the attention of the appropriate state agency any child about whom I even have suspicions of emotional or social deprivation or neglect or child battering. As the mother of Alex and Chrissy, I have very strong suspicions that they are now in a situation of deprivation and fear. I cannot, however, make an ordinary health-worker's report for them. The agency representatives whom I talked to today said they could not get involved in "an ordinary marital dispute," even though they agreed that the children were most probably in at least psychological danger. And worse, there is no national network of child-abuse agencies; all are for individual states. If I knew where the children were now, I could perhaps get some help from the agency in that state, I was told.

Paul has now served divorce papers by publication, by printing a notice in a local newspaper three weeks in a row. More publicity for me and the children! Paul is also worried about that method of service—worried about some legal technicality I can hardly believe, that Michael could claim he didn't know the divorce was happening because he was not in this area at the time of publication. I cannot understand why his lawyer and mine cannot simply testify that we all met together to discuss the terms of a divorce. Now we must wait several more weeks before there can even be a preliminary hearing—at which time I will get legal custody of the children. Paul warns that my custody of Alex and Chrissy may not be honored in another state if they are absent at the time of the preliminary hearing.

Paul explains to me that when (if) we do find Michael and Alex and Chris, there may have to be a new custody determination in the court of the state where they are found. There is even, apparently, some slight risk here in Minnesota that I might lose in a custody contest. According to Paul, there is always risk in taking a custody question to a judge because it depends on the momentary mood of the judge and whether she or he is willing to hear both sides out, what her or his particular biases are, how she or he is touched by the presentation of evidence and arguments, and whether she or he feels that a favor is owed to one or the other of the attorneys. Surely, then, that risk would be greater if the custody hearing were heard in a strange place. I would have to find a new attorney (while here I have the good fortune of having the help of a respected and honest lawyer of good reputation), would have to be examined by another psychiatrist if my suicide gesture were brought into the contest, would be alone in a strange place, would have to give up my work for a while. What would happen to Mary during that time? Would she have to leave school and come with me? I have no kin with whom she could stay, and I am not sure that I could ask that great a favor of friends. Alex and Christopher would be placed in a foster home during the period of the custody determination, Paul believes. The whole process sounds terrible.

I go to sleep every night thinking of Chrissy and Alexy as babies—nursing and learning to eat from a spoon and toddling about, getting into things. Alex used to have magnificent temper tantrums—he used to know just how to hit his head on the cupboard door so that it made a great rattling noise while not really hurting himself. Chris in his long, white, knit baby night-gown and his flaming red hair looked like Casper the ghost. Alex learned early to throw and catch a ball, his perseverance standing him in good stead as he practiced and practiced and got to be very good. Each was a spectacle with chicken pox, covered from head to foot. Alex always loved the music from music-box stuffed animals, and Chris always took the mechanism apart to see how it worked. The pair once got into some green paint that I was using to paint chairs, smearing their hands and faces and feet and then pulling down their pants to give themselves green dinkers as well, shrieking with giggly delight. Each always wanted a lullaby and a "lie down wis' me" at bedtime. These are the kinds of memories that, for the older children, I treasure when they come into my head. But for the little ones I go over and over their short lives, compulsively, trying to reconstruct every detail of the past that is all I have and know of them now. It is as if time were stopped, their future lives cut short. Often I cry myself to sleep.

SUNDAY, APRIL 18, EASTER SUNDAY: Michael called today. He let me talk with the little boys. They had been carefully coached—each said the same little speech to me. "We ain't comin' back. We're never goin' to live in your house again. We're goin' to get ou'selves a new mommy." I was nearly silenced, in sorrow and rage. I told them both that I would always be their mommy, and that I loved them very much. At the end of the conversation Michael screamed his usual abuse at me: I was responsible for all that was happening to us, employed mothers deserved no child-support payments, the divorce courts were uniformly unfair to men, I was an unfit mother and dangerous to my children, I was a greedy bitch.

I put down the telephone and howled in pain and frustration. I nearly collided with Jason, coming to find me. He had listened to the entire conversation on the other phone and was shocked and stunned. Until now, Jason had only known of my angry and sad reactions to Michael's phone calls. He had heard me out, but reacted with some ambivalence, resenting my reaction, and perhaps even disbelieving. Now he was pale. There were tears in his eyes.

"I can't believe what he said to you. You know, he must have told the little boys what to say, because they both sounded like they were reciting pieces." Jason held me, put my head on his shoulder. "He is vicious, those were terrible things he said. But you know, he can't really poison the way the boys feel about you. They love you and they know you're their mommy. *And we're going to find them and bring them back."*

I would not have chosen for Jason to hear that awful tirade— I would have thought that he needed to be protected from the worst of the venom. But as it turned out, Jason's mind eased after that morning. He no longer felt there was no right and wrong to the dilemma or that he had to remain neutral. Hearing Michael brought about Jason's alliance with the younger children and with me. Some of his own inner misery seemed to lighten, and he became from that day on an active supporter in what was to be a prolonged, sad, and difficult struggle.

This year of maturity, of separation from home and family, is a terribly difficult time for Jason to deal with his father's behavior. Until now, he has managed his own pain in this affair by a sullen withdrawal and a superficial playfulness that conceals his misery only a little. Today, for the first time, Jason and I can talk about Jason. Before now, he has always turned our talks into a concern for me—he has been very sensitive to my bad times, very careful to urge me to call a friend or visit with Meg when I felt discouraged and down. Today Jason can tell me how much he is hurting.

In the first few weeks after Michael left, Jason asked several times about the inheritance of craziness. He feels the pressure of being the only left-behind child who is biologically Michael's. I tried to reassure him that the irrationality that is more and more in evidence in Michael's calls and letters, and the acts of child stealing, are not directly inherited. We have talked about the kinds of early childhood experiences that could predispose one to an adult repetition of a father's (and a grandfather's) craziness. We had agreed that Jason is not likely to be directly hurt by all of this, at least not in the way that Alexy and Chrissy are being hurt. (I once asked Michael, during one of his telephone calls, if he wanted to risk harming his sons in such a way that they might grow up to a third generation of this sort of raging retribution. He said, "Maybe.")

But until today Jason has denied that he wished Michael would come back for him, that he needed him. We agreed that it is good that Jason is partly out of the family, at school in Minneapolis. He needs to get to know and trust some adult men who are even-tempered and sensitive, prudent and responsible.

Hearing what Michael said today on the phone and what he had instructed the little boys to say to me, Jason now disclaims any connection to what Michael is as being too foreign to Jason's nature, too excessive for Jason's repertoire. Jason has now moved off dead center and away from his split allegiance. But I don't think he has lost his sympathetic pain at Michael's distress. On the one hand, I am sorry about this—I have tried very hard not to ask Jason to take sides. On the other hand, if it eases Jason to see the struggle in this new light—even if only by allowing him to talk about how sad he feels for himself—then I count this a good turn of events.

I think I shall discontinue my present telephone number and get a new, unlisted number. I am absolutely at the mercy of Michael's calls and am undone by his venom when he does call. He uses his calls to relieve his own boredom, to maintain contact with me, but never to give me information that I could use to end this mess. And since I so rarely even get to talk to Alexy and Chrissy, the calls have almost no usefulness for me or for the little boys. Perhaps cutting that route of communication would precipitate Michael's return.

One consequence of a decision to change my phone number would be that I would be less accessible to any of my friends who might contact me by telephone. Their calls are a major source of support for me. I notice, though, that there are fewer and fewer calls, not because my friends are less caring and supportive but because the whole affair is terribly painful to them as well. Two of them have spoken about this directly; they want so much to believe that this tragic affair has ended, and they feel so personally torn by grief at the children's absence that they "forget" about calling or postpone making contact. One said, "In a funny way, we must ask you to comfort us, to tell us that the grief is endurable and that the pain will soon end."

Our combined helplessness is frustrating and angering—there ought to be some way to find those three and bring them back! For those of my friends who are mothers, or who know my children well, or who work with small children, there is a real sharing of pain, a sense that our collective worst fears have come true. I hear in their voices a need to be reassured by me that we will find ways to take effective action and to return Chris and Alex.

Paul and I have been talking at some length about what Paul calls "self-help," meaning some action outside of or beside the usual legal channels. Specifically, we have talked about hiring some extra-legal assistance to find the children and bring them back. All of my inquiries have pointed to Pinkerton's as the most effective and reliable finders. I have been told that Pinkerton's agents may not be able or willing to return the children to their home; Paul has suggested that he has contacts that could direct us to someone who would do that.

I am so torn on this question. If it is wrong, as I know it is, for Michael to tear the children from their home, their brother and sister, and from me, it is also wrong—although I think to a lesser degree—for me to return them in an equally unforeseen manner. For Alex and Chris, a sudden unexpected return, perhaps accompanied by a stranger, must be just one more episode in which they feel like pawns of adults who control their lives without their permission.

It becomes a question of choosing the lesser wrong. I know well enough what Michael's ordinary relationship with children is. I can imagine what is happening to them now that he is so torn apart with anger, grief, and retributive energy. I am nearly ready to decide that there would be less harm to them if they could be found and returned home in one smooth operation than if they continue to roam as captives with Michael.

Paul has continued to hope until this week that we would succeed in finding some legal and official mechanism to search for them and secure their return. Now he is discouraged and is beginning to talk more vigorously about using some self-help methods. His inquiries have also pointed to Pinkerton's as the most likely source of help. On his instructions I prepare a fact sheet—descriptions, photographs, information about the car, and the name, address, and description of every contact person I can imagine that Michael might use.

Michael has no close friends. His dependence on me as his only active friend has been one of the unbearable binds of the marriage. But he had two friends when he was in the Navy, long before I met him, and he has continued to have very intermittent contact with them, perhaps two or three letters or phone calls in the twenty years since they were close.

I have called both of them, wondering if they would give me any information if Michael had made contact with them recently. One, a lawyer, admits to having seen Michael and the boys and is very cagey with me over the telephone. He is insinuating something accusatory but not saying it straight; he implies that he thinks Michael could get custody of the boys. Has Michael convinced him that I am neglectful? I suppose that people who do not know me, who have not seen the quality of my relationships with my children, might be taken in by Michael's ranting.

The other friend had not seen Michael and was very sympathetic and distressed over the telephone; he told me he was very sorry to hear what had happened. He asked if *I* knew that Michael was repeating what Michael's own father had done to him. But at the end of the conversation I was not convinced that he would notify me if he heard from Michael. The bonds of loyalty from those old friendships are very strong indeed.

Those are the only contact people I can think of, other than Michael's father, sister, and brother. I do not know Michael's family very well. He has always been very distant from and disdainful of them. The only time our families have visited together in the last ten years—which was two years ago—Michael's sister took me aside and told me how astounded she was that Michael's marriage had lasted. She said, "I always thought that he was too self-centered and impatient and uncaring to be a husband and father." Her remark gave me a jolt; I was then beginning to think more and more seriously about the possibility of divorce, and I didn't know how to answer her. I smiled weakly, but I did not contradict her.

Now, however, I think that his family may have closed ranks around Michael. I have talked to a close friend of theirs by telephone. She is a nice lady and sorrows for the little boys, whom she remembers well from our visit there. She says, however, that the family excludes her carefully and pointedly from all their conversations about Michael and his present affairs. They all think he is the smartest, most successful, and richest of them all and that he must be doing the right thing.

Paul will arrange for a conference between himself, a Pinkerton's representative, and me some day later this week. I will in the meantime wrestle with my own doubts about the advisability of using self-help measures.

Mary's teacher called me in last week to talk about Mary's school situation. I looked forward to that conversation with dread —I did not want to hear that Mary's hurts were showing in school. But what her teacher wanted to tell me was that she was delighted with a change in Mary in the past few weeks—she didn't know what might have happened, but her life seemed to have brightened. Everything was going better for her—peer relationships, academic work, sports, and her relationships with adults.

I reflected then on something that I had not paid enough attention to—my own sense of the peace, fresh air, and sunshine in our household since Michael has gone. Despite our grief over missing Chris and Alex, and our distress at Michael's misery and the pain he is determined to visit on us, we have become a more peaceful and mutually supportive family. I am certain that Mary's school behavior is significant of her release from Michael's personal attacks, accusations of stupidity, and unpredictable rages. She is becoming better able to define herself and to trust that she can predict her environment and conduct herself with safety and confidence, as indeed she seems to be doing. Jason, like Mary, is also doing better now in his academic work.

I have been told that there is a belief among some townsfolk that I must not care about the boys, else why have I not simply found them and brought them back? Some apparently have assumed that I must believe I could not have their custody, taking my tolerance of their absence as evidence. Perhaps I should talk more and with more people about my desperate efforts to find them. I have been very reticent, out of a sense of privacy and a self-protective concealment of the intensity of my pain, about talking about this.

I continue to be angry at the rumors that Michael has spread about me in this town. I suspect that anyone who knows me cannot believe the things he has said. But despite the fact that the patients who come to our office seem well pleased with the service we give, we are not seeing as many new patients as we think we should be. I begin to wonder if our practice can survive these rumors, in this area where there are already several physicians practicing in my field. In this town the subtle prejudice against women professionals is very enduring, reflecting the underlying conservatism of most of the residents. I have worked hard and invested much of myself in my practice, as have the three women that I work with. I begin to have an inkling that I may lose that too.

WEDNESDAY, APRIL 28: They have been gone almost eight weeks. I have dreams about the boys now—car crashes and drownings. Once I dreamed that Alex got off the bus in front of our house with a tag around his neck, "Please Return to . . ." I have been reading about Sojourner Truth and how her five-year-old was sold as a slave, and how she got him back through legal means, and how when he finally came back to her he was covered with scars. He was by then so afraid of being hurt further that he followed the instructions of his master and said to the judge that he didn't recognize his mother, and he lied at first about how he had gotten his scars.

This story and the classic myth about Ceres, whose child Proserpina was stolen by Pluto, god of the underworld, remind me that there is in this situation a Common Woman theme. The kidnaping of our children is a threat that we all live with, a pain that cuts away at our very hearts, a loss that calls forth every reserve of strength and wit and courage.

All the stories I have been hearing about children similarly kidnaped in recent times fire my fantasy and make me weep for mothers. We mothers don't want our children to be our slaves, to make a profit from them, or to own them. The old legal convention that children are property seems to me to be a denial of their humanity. We never own our children but only cherish them in trust for their safe passage through childhood.

I am reminded of the current and age-old abortion controversy. Those who forbid a woman to choose whether or not she will bear a child often argue that the conceptus "belongs to" the future father, or even to "the fathers of society." The mother's responsibility is to feed and to care for and to keep safe. And shame and pity on her if she does not elect to connect herself to a man for support, to sell her services for society's approval of her mothering.

Once I, like so many women, believed that we could best pursue our own self-respect and self-interest by carefully putting our energies into situations where it seemed that women had some advantage. The privilege of caring for small children was clearly an area where men were commonly deprived, by social custom and by their own early upbringing and their expectations of what was acceptable "manly" behavior. I was one of those women who argued that men should know the pleasures of child care. I believed that if fathers were urged to learn to become attached to their small children they would benefit by ceasing to regard children as property, their children would benefit by having more than one active parent, and women would benefit in the end by gaining a more equitable position in society. We women could not, I thought, ask for equity for ourselves until we had given over our own few disproportionate advantages.

Certainly in my own marriage I worked to teach Michael to spend time with our children and to become attached to them. With Chrissy, Michael took an active role in child care from his birth, never as much as I but certainly more than he had done with any of the older children. I believe now that Michael and many other fathers I have heard about only *added* a sense of attachment to their persistent sense of property-ownership.

I also remember attending a meeting of attorneys and public officials on the subject of child custody—specifically about the question of the rights of fathers to custody after marital separation. I had not thought much then about the pain for a mother of losing custody. I suspect I always assumed that we were considering situations where both parents agreed that fathers should have custody, but judges were unreasonably following the traditional assumption that mothers were always and naturally the most capable parents. The lawyer sitting next to me leaned over and whispered, "More and more fathers are going to get custody of their children. That should stop some of these women who just want to walk out the front door on their marriages." I got a glimpse then of men's use of the custody of children as a weapon of anger against their wives.

I stopped going to those meetings and supporting the priority of change in that admittedly pro-woman bit of discrimination. I am now convinced that the so-called "maternal presumption," the tendency of judges to assume that mothers are usually more suitable as care-taking parents than fathers, is one of the few scraps of favoritism that we women have. We should not give it over lightly until we have in fact reached a more equitable position in other areas of our lives—the economic, occupational, educational, legal, and so on. We should have learned by now not to be so ready to turn over half of our blue marbles before we have some reasonable evidence that the red marbles and the yellow ones and the green ones are also going to be divied up.

We are, of course, also hurt by the maternal presumption and the attached belief that parenting is instinctive for us, that it is mindless activity requiring little energy or thought. The opportunity to care for our children is one of the few genuinely pleasurable privileges we women have and must not be given over to men except with great caution.

Paul and I met with the regional Pinkerton's chief two days ago. Paul thought first off to ask Mr. Kenniston to check and see whether Michael might have hired Pinkerton's himself. We have entered the resource of self-help as a means of retrieving the boys, but both Paul and I still have strong reservations about the correctness of that decision.

Kenniston was at pains to tell us several times that the agency was not allowed, by charter, to do investigative work in divorce cases. It took me some time to realize that he was talking about not wanting to be asked to report to me if Michael was found with another woman. I finally laughed—I have known for some time that if Michael fell in love with another woman much of his pain in the divorce would be eased.

We finally got past Kenniston's misapprehension and convinced him that it was only the children, not the fugitive husband, who were the objects of the requested search. We talked about how impossible, and how impossibly expensive, it would be to search unless we had some reasonable idea of where they might be. The charges were to be $15 per hour per investigator, plus expenses. Paul did some quick arithmetic and announced that in a few days we could accumulate costs of $1,000. In fact, the actual costs ran up much more quickly after we began the search process.

Kenniston asked for a letter guaranteeing a payment of $2,000 before Pinkerton's could agree to begin a search. He would begin by trying to get information from the central (national) offices of the major credit-card companies about Michael's record of credit-card charges.

In the two days since that meeting Kenniston has not answered our preliminary questions. I suppose Paul or I will have to call him back. I shall ask Paul to do that. I think that in situations like this his male voice has more commanding authority than mine. I hate that fact of my life, but I have learned to use it.

Every now and then, in my odd moments of repose, I am overwhelmed by my astonishment at the accusation of "unfit mother." That Michael should claim that of me is the most shocking rupture of our trust. I have not dared to think about it very much—the merest hint of that threat and I get a little breathless and sweaty. As I begin to look more closely at my anxiety, I begin to realize that it is because we all know, in our heart of hearts, that we are unfit mothers.

Being a mother, dealing fairly and intelligently and humanly with a growing small child, must be one of the most challenging, difficult, impossible-of-success jobs in the universe. Impossible of success partly because our society never credits us if our children do well, for then it is said that the child is clearly good material. Yet, we are readily blamed if anything goes wrong—from unhappiness in the child, to acting out, poor work in school subjects, bothering the neighbors, being "late" with toilet training, getting sick, or deciding not to go to college. (The blame/credit balance is changing a little now, in a pretty unhealthy way, with all of the "bad seed" and "devil possession" books and movies about small children as evil-from-the-start. That kind of finger-pointing is only the other side of our need in this society to *blame* and offers no comfort at all to a mother who wants to help her children grow to be strong and self-respecting.)

Given the expectations placed on mothers—if we do everything right the product will be perfect, or if the product is found imperfect we must have done something wrong—it is impossible for mothering ever to be successful. Given a more tolerant and human view of mothers and children and their connection in child rearing, we would all be able to admit that we can only do our best, and that we make mistakes with the best of intentions—fail to hear what the child wants or needs, act too quickly, are too tired to respond as we wish we could, and so on. In that sense we are all "unfit" mothers, and we know that. We want so much to be good for our children, but the kind of goodness they can use and we hope to give seems beyond human capabilities.

Not that I think it is a bad thing for us to hold up to ourselves some ideal about the process of mothering—some notion of being always able to listen, always willing to take time, always wise enough to go back over what we have done or said to make the corrections that will be more supportive, more respectful of the child and of ourselves. It is only that we ourselves, mothers, know that real/ideal discrepancy and understand its origins. We should not have to expect that some outsider, some judge or investigator who may never have lived the role of twenty-four-hour-a-day parent, will presume to decide about our fitness.

I know simultaneously that I am a fit mother in the legal sense—a damn good mother—and an unfit mother by my own standards. But my own standards are unattainable: I understand that and accept it with the grace and laughter that mothers share. I hold to those standards because I think that for the most part they help me to do my best with my children. I just don't want uncomprehending outsiders, strangers who are not mothers, comparing me to my standards.

Nor do I want to be compared to the "ideal mother" standards of our sentimental and woman-hating society. The mother of every man's dream (which is never the dream of a woman, knowing what mothering is like) is someone who is always there, always giving, never withholding, never depriving—except of course when she must keep the children restrained so as not to disturb the father. No woman ever attains that vision, and as real-life mothers who care about our children we know that we wouldn't even want to be like that. Among other things, we would, if we followed those dictates, fail to teach our children to understand about give-and-take, collaboration, caring for others, the reciprocity of needs.

I shudder at the accusation of unfit mother because I know that if my mothering is closely examined I cannot meet the test of my own standards, nor can I meet the test of the idealized good-virgin-mother of our society's mythology. And at the same time I know, fiercely and with anger, that I *am* good for my children. But how does one ever prove that?

How would it be proved that I were unfit? *There* lies the kernel of Michael's broken trust. Only someone who has lived with me could know that I took a great risk with Jason when I taught him to read when he was a troubled and dyslexic first-grader; that I probably weaned Mary before she was ready to give up her bottle; that I am frustrated and impatient with the mixed autonomy/babyishness of five-year-olds. All those years that Michael said he respected and admired my way with children—was he taking notes on my flaws?

I am told that in most states there are three common grounds of presumption for an "unfit mother" decision: prostitution, drug or alcohol abuse, and lesbianism. Is that why Michael began to broadcast the information that I must be a lesbian? That label simultaneously provides him with an explanation for my disillusionment as his wife—a face-saver—and at the same time lays the groundwork for a custody contest. Even the courts are now recognizing that sexual preference is unrelated to mothering performance.

"Child of my body, bone of my bone, apple of my eye." The song is cathartic for me—every time I listen I cry bitter tears. Meg leaves the room when I put the record on the phonograph. She cannot bear to look at my grief.

Meg's friendship, and the sustenance of all my friends, has saved my sanity throughout these weeks. But there are still private moments of grief that can't really be shared—depths that I can't explain or put to words and that are indescribably painful for others to glimpse.

I have been thinking about ways I might use publicity to help find the boys. I have talked to a friend who writes for the Minneapolis newspaper; she recently did a column on kidnaped children and encouraged me to let her try to do something about the boys, perhaps even a piece that would get picked up on the wire services. She and I have known each other for a long time, have shared information about day care and women's employment and women's health issues. Other friends tell me, however, that I am overly optimistic, that she would never be able to publish the kind of information that would be needed to find them: descriptions, my own telephone number, and so on. I am also rather mistrustful of those sorts of press contacts. What if part of the story were misquoted, or left out? What if the story led readers to hide Michael and the children? What if it were distorted in another way and I were subject to a libel suit? Newspapers never let you see their copy before they print it. For now, at least, I have decided not to do this, despite my friend's urging. Paul believes that it might be useful, and I may change my mind later.

Jason's mood has lightened and his self-respect grown. Mary goes on as if her life were pretty much in order. This feels like a moment of quiet in our siege, a time when we should be gathering strength.

I think that I will urge Paul to tell Pinkerton's to look at the addresses we have for Michael's family and friends. It will probably be just a very expensive fishing expedition. But with the loss of telephone contact since I changed my phone number, I feel haunted by my helplessness and need to take some definitive action. I may use all my savings in this venture, but I can't think of anything more important to use that money for than to find Christopher and Alex.

FETCHING

THURSDAY, MAY 6: They are found! I can hardly believe it. It took until yesterday to get clearance, payments, and contacts settled with Pinkerton's, and their investigators started checking those addresses today.

Paul called me at my office, a little after noon. The car—but so far not Michael, Alex and Chris—has been spotted at Michael's sister's house just outside St. Louis. The investigator was going to keep the car under surveillance. No sooner had I begun to digest this information—what, indeed, was I to do now?—when Paul called again to say that in the interval of the investigator's reporting phone call the car had disappeared. Now with two investigators in two cars on the scene—but, apparently no telephones in their cars—Michael's car is once again parked outside the house, and Michael and the two boys were seen going inside. What next?

The decision about using self-help to go for the boys seems to have been made for us. In my own mind, at least, I cannot know where they are and not make every effort to bring Alex and Chris home. I am aware of putting into the back of my mind all of my worries about the propriety and rightness of that decision. I feel driven, almost as if by a force outside myself, to send someone for them or to go myself.

Paul and I have simply not thought through this eventuality to a clear plan. Kenniston has been very definite with Paul; he checked with the highest authorities in the Pinkerton's agency (apparently this task is not yet a routine assignment for them) and has been told that under no circumstances will a Pinkerton's agent assist in retrieving the boys, even with the custody order given me in court two weeks ago after notice by publication. Although I know that my fetching the boys is entirely lawful, that decision by the proper and respected Pinkerton's agency makes me feel a little queasy, as if I were proposing to do something that was shady.

Should I simply go there myself? Paul is also undecided; he talks with Tom Brown, the senior attorney in his firm. Tom's first reaction is that self-help is the least preferable alternative. We might request that a local sheriff detain them. Paul explains to me that that would almost certainly mean a custody hearing there in Missouri, with delays for court time, the boys put into foster care, and always that distant, improbable, but very frightening possibility that because Michael has had them with him for so many weeks he might be awarded custody. Then there is the necessity of an appeal, and so on.

Paul is also deeply concerned about my personal safety. Whenever I have talked to Clarence, Michael's one acquaintance in this town, he has told me that if Michael should return here unexpectedly I should be sure to have adequate protection. He really thinks that Michael might have homicidal intentions toward me. It is astonishing to hear that someone might have such ill will toward me (especially someone who, in Clarence's words, "still loves" me), but both women friends and Paul have urged me to take those warnings very seriously.

The third alternative is to hire an agent to retrieve the children. Paul could find such a person, through contacts—someone whom he describes as an "underworld type." What physical and psychological trauma do I then risk for the children? It seems to me that such an agent would only escalate the possibility of violence. And I do not want to think about the puzzlement and distress of Alex and Chrissy if they were snatched by a stranger, even one who told them that he was returning them to their mommy.

I feel certain that I must go myself. Paul and Tom are still debating their recommendation; the day is coming to an end. At last report from Pinkerton's, the three and their car are still at that house.

I pace through the evening in an agony of indecision. I am only certain that now that I have found them I must do something about bringing them back.

FRIDAY, MAY 7: Paul is still the contact with Kenniston, but I am increasingly uncomfortable about the long chain we have established for information transfer. The investigator in St. Louis reports to his superior who reports to Kenniston who reports to Paul who reports to me. I cannot get directly any of the information I would need to plan to fetch the children, and I fear we could lose or distort information along that long chain. I am beginning to feel that I must go there to find out directly whether the boys *can* be rescued.

Nothing more of significance was reported to have happened at the sister's house last night. The boys were seen playing outside, without jackets in a chilly rain, under the eyes of their two teenage cousins. Michael was apparently away from the house in his car while they were playing outside, a relatively easy situation for a rescue operation. This morning Michael, Alex, Chris, and Michael's sister were followed on a long shopping expedition. They are back at the house now and Kenniston wants instructions on how to proceed.

Tom Brown told Paul today that he believes that to have the boys picked up by a hired agent would prejudice the judge against me in any future court proceedings. Paul, on the other hand, is still very worried about my physical safety if I go there myself.

I feel that a decision must be made, and I shall make it. I will go there myself with help from friends, will assess the situation at first hand, and will pick up the boys if that is at all possible and return them to their home. Paul and Tom Brown now advise me to go; they feel that the judges of our district court will not count this against me. I will heed Paul's warnings about physical danger to myself but will focus my attention on not putting the boys into any real danger.

I call Jason, who offered to rescue the boys when he was last here visiting for the weekend. I also call Eve, my trusted friend, who works well with me, gets along easily with Jason, and is a cool-headed planner in a crisis. Both are willing to go with me; we agree that we will plan the contingencies of the actual pickup as we travel.

I suspect that our best opportunity will come when Michael goes out on some errand, leaving the boys at the house. Weekend days are a less likely time for that sort of separation of Michael from the boys than are week days. We agree to travel on Sunday, gather our information on Sunday night, and wait on Monday for an opportunity to get the boys. I am mindful of the fact that once we arrive on the scene we will lose the assistance of the Pinkerton's investigators.

Jason will be missing school, Eve will miss work. This is a gigantic effort for them to make. Am I also asking them to risk personal violence? I can hardly bear to think about that possibility.

SATURDAY, MAY 8TH: I have spent this day getting ready to travel and trying to think through what is likely to happen when we arrive. I vacillate between thinking that I am making overly elaborate plans, influenced by spy stories, and that I am not sufficiently experienced in such an affair to be able to plan for all contingencies.

Kenniston was instructed yesterday to report directly to me, thus cutting one person out of that information chain. I must do what has to be done without any direct help from Paul. I know that Paul will be available if I need to call him for advice. I have heard no news from Kenniston all day.

Ann has lent me a magnificent old Army jacket with all kinds of snap pockets—I pack the pockets as I would my purse. We have air reservations to leave early tomorrow morning, to transfer in Chicago and travel on to St. Louis. We can rent a car there

—or perhaps we should have two cars, so that we can transfer after we have picked up the boys—and can drive to the suburb where Michael's sister lives.

My friend Beth has planned for some time to come here for a visit. She will come this weekend, staying here to keep the household in order and to be available for Mary. Meg and her daughter Molly have also offered to stay at the house; Meg will tie together all communications at this home base for the operation. We get a little giggly planning this torch-and-dagger scheme; nothing in my past has ever prepared me to be a secret agent or to run a risk of genuine physical danger. But all of my motherhood demands that I do whatever has to be done to rescue my children.

Mary knows all about the mission—she is noticing and curious and I find it impossible to lie to her about so important an event. She is very apprehensive about the possibility of physical danger to me, both, I think, because she knows Michael and senses or fears his potential for physical violence and because I am now Mary's only available parent and any risk to my safety is very frightening. But she believes that she has a right to know what is happening and would, I think, be even more frightened knowing that something of importance was afoot but not being told the truth. Beth and Meg are both tremendously fond of Mary and will do their best to hold her together during my absence. Of course she wishes that she could come, too.

Kenniston calls at midnight. I have been pestering his answering service all day, angry that I have had no report during this long and expensive day of surveillance. He reports on the activities of Michael and the boys up until supper time; there is nothing very helpful in his briefing—the three went out for one errand, all together, it rained most of the day, the little boys have not been seen since midafternoon. Clearly I must go there to get some useful idea of whether or not it will be possible to get the boys.

I am restless, excited, more than a little apprehensive. I have $300 in cash, all I could muster, plus my own credit cards. Beth lets me use one of her credit cards, in case we think we should not use our own names. I go to bed at 1:30—I will need to get up at 6:30 to make the long drive to the airport. I lie awake, planning, then get up with a start. I have not wanted even to hope that we might really be successful in getting the boys. I go out to the car and put two pillows, the boys' own little favorite nap blankets, some graham crackers, and a thermos of grape juice in the back of my car. If I bring them back I will drive directly north to Jo's lake cabin, a place Michael doesn't know about.

I try to sleep.

SUNDAY, MAY 9TH, 3:00 A.M.: Kenniston just called, waking me out of a deep sleep. I do not think very well when I am first awakened. Meg and Beth both heard the telephone ring and came to sit in my bedroom.

Kenniston reports that Michael has apparently learned that he is being watched. He put Chris and Alex into the car at 11:30, a little over three hours ago, and drove for two hours on back country roads at high speeds, the Pinkerton's investigator following the whole way. After that he returned the boys to his sister's house and drove in the same fashion in his sister's car, again being followed. He came out to the Pinkerton's investigator and shouted angrily that if he continued to be followed he would call the police—which of course he could not do. Then he drove his own car out again, again without the boys, and this time he dumped his car in a ditch—he was not hurt but the front end of the car was badly damaged. There was then some flurry of activity at his sister's house before the lights went out.

Kenniston tells me now that it was highly unlikely that they could maintain an unnoticed surveillance for so long a time, especially in a residential area. I wish I had been told that before we planned the timetable that we are now on. Probably we should have gone down there on Thursday, when they were first spotted.

Beth, Meg, and I try to figure out what all of this means. It is impossible to know whether they are still there, whether Michael's awareness of the surveillance will make it impossible for us to get the children, whether his potential for violence is heightened.

I feel as if our course of action has been set in motion, that we must go or I will never forgive myself for having bypassed an opportunity to retrieve them. I don't think that I can properly understand the situation until we are actually and physically there. Meg and Beth and I begin to be uproariously silly, sitting in the dark of the night with only a candle burning, very tired and keyed up. We agree that the plans should proceed and return to our beds for a few more hours of sleep.

SUNDAY, MAY 9, 11:00 P.M.: We have arrived in St. Louis. Sitting in our motel, registered under Beth's name, Eve, Jason, and I are somewhere between matter-of-fact and in-a-dream. We have laid all the plans we can think of for tomorrow and must now try to get some rest.

We met at the airport early this morning, feeling self-conscious and rather preposterous. From my Army jacket and running shoes to Jason's knapsack full of schoolbooks to Eve's purse with a frilly nightgown ("for the comfort of my soul"), we suspect that every-one who sees us must know that we are up to something very, very strange. We try very hard to be nonchalant.

At the stopover in Chicago we go to the airport drugstore. When we had started on the airplane to plan how we might pull off our caper we realized we couldn't "synchronize our watches" because both Eve and Jason had forgotten theirs. We choose a watch for each (Do we need to pay for a watch with a date? What are the cheapest watches that will fit? What does the clerk think of us, anyway?) and then choose three pocket flashlights. I pay for them with my own charge card and the clerk says with elaborate formality, "Thank you very much, *Doctor!*" As we saunter out of the store, stifling giggles, Jason says, "Having purchased time and light, we now go in search of truth."

We talk on the plane about our hope that there might be access to the house through woods. Apparently the house is at the end of a short dead-end street, which makes it difficult for the investi-gators to watch. Eve could drive, and Jason and I could each pick up one of the boys. Is changing cars a necessary safety precaution? We will need a map to plan how to get out of the state and away from Missouri state police as fast as possible. Will Michael claim that the children have been kidnaped by strangers? I have several copies of the custody order with me. I could drop them in the street as we drive away, even though I know the order is technically valid only in the state of Minnesota. Jason says he feels perfectly comfortable about confronting Michael's sister in her house —"All right, let's cut out this nonsense; these children need to be with their mother and brother and sister"—if Michael is gone and the children are inside the house. Finally we are overcome by the realization that we are planning in a vacuum of information, and we stop talking and ride the rest of the way to St. Louis in silence.

When we land in St. Louis we rent two cars, both in my name, using my charge card. None of us has any very good sense about how much secrecy we should use. The clerk asks where we will be returning the cars—it makes some difference in the billing procedure—and I hem and haw and say here at this office. I am a lousy liar and a lousy actress.

We follow each other with our two cars to a motel that seems to be close to the neighborhood of Michael's sister's house. I have the home phone number of the local Pinkerton's supervisor. He is waiting to hear from me. He will talk to the head investigator within the hour and will tell him to come here to meet us.

Alan, the Pinkerton's man, arrives in a car full of empty fast-food containers and fancy portable radio equipment. He can talk to another of the investigators (there are now three on the scene) but not to his supervisor. He explains that neither Michael nor the children have been seen all day. No one knows whether they are still there, in hiding, whether they are just spending an ordinary quiet Sunday in the house, or whether they have left. Alan has a hunch they have left.

Alan drives us to a place near the house where we meet a second investigator, Ellie. Both Alan and Ellie have been on duty for more than forty-eight hours and are exhausted. There are no other Pinkerton's investigators available in this area to relieve the three now on duty.

The house is located not only at the end of a dead-end road

but also deep in one of those suburban housing developments designed to keep strangers out. Strange cars are likely to be readily noticed—Alan was reported by residents to the local police within hours after he arrived, but was able to reassure the police that he was a Pinkerton's investigator on a routine assignment. Alan and Ellie think that it would be unwise for us to drive into the development and near the house tonight. They drive us around the development, and we can see that there is an approach to the house through a little woods.

One more bit of information, the most sobering of all: Michael has never left the house without taking Alex and Chrissy with him. Unless he is separated from the little boys, it will be very difficult for us to get to them without risking his violent reaction.

We return to the motel. I call Meg, who will report to Paul. We still have not settled the question of whether we might want the assistance of Paul's contact, the "underworld type" who would help pick up the boys. I presume that his role would be to distract or restrain Michael, were that necessary. I feel a strong revulsion to the possibility of violence, especially with the thought that Alex or Chrissy might get hurt. Meg says that Mary is openly worried about my safety and torn by her hope that the boys can be rescued. I talk to Mary and reassure her that I will not put myself or Jason or Eve in a situation of risk, and also that we will do our very best to get the boys. Meg says, and I believe, that the stress of being the one left to coordinate the caper at home is a terrible burden.

We cannot plan any more until morning.

MONDAY, MAY 10TH, 5:00 P.M.: Alan called at the motel at 9:00 this morning. He had spoken to several neighbors—most would not talk to him but one said that she feared there might be a child stealer sheltered in the neighborhood. A neighbor living next to Michael's sister's house said that she believed that the father and the two little boys who had been visiting had left the night before, apparently stealing out through the very woods we had planned to lurk in to wait for a chance to pick up the boys. She thinks that Chrissy and Alex were carried through the woods in the middle of Saturday night to another neighbor's house, and that the three might have been driven away on a road that the Pinkerton's people were not watching. Michael's disabled car remains at his sister's house.

None of this is certain, only conjecture and hearsay; I suppose it could even be a planted story to get us to go away. Alan suggests that Michael's sister's house should be searched and his sister questioned. For that we will need to go through the local court and start a proceeding that might end in a custody hearing here in this state. I do know that I will in the end have their custody, and I have no doubt that I am the parent best able to care for them appropriately. If we must risk a custody hearing in this state, then so be it.

Meg has a cousin in St. Louis. She calls him and describes our problem, asking him for the name of a good and reputable lawyer. I call the office of the firm that he suggests, and speak immediately to the young lawyer who "handles this type of case." He is courteous and sounds willing to help; he offers me an appointment in an hour. I call Paul, explain the situation, and ask him to call the attorney here to fill him in on the problem.

I worry now that I will frighten the lawyer, judge, sheriff, and any one else I might meet, dressed as I am for a running-in-the-woods commando action. Jason, Eve, and I go first to a department store and buy an entire set of clothes, from the skin out. Eve says that it is truly an "adorable outfit," that I look very much the suburban housewife.

The young lawyer is very helpful. He listens to the story, draws up papers for temporary custody, and he and I wander around in the courthouse until he finds the family court judge who signs the papers. The lawyer tells me all about his marriage and his two adopted children. We arrange to meet the sheriff in the neighborhood; he will search the house if he needs to, in an effort to serve the custody papers.

The sheriff looks every bit like a small-town cop. He questions me, asks if I think there might be resistance, violence, or the use of guns. I tell him that I don't know. He orders me not to come near the house when he goes to search. I learn at the end of the conversation that he has thought that I am the first wife of Michael's sister's husband—the sheriff knows all the local folk by reputation. Eve and Jason and I giggle, wondering if he would have brought out the two teenaged cousins, the wrong children.

The sheriff and the lawyer go to the house with their court order. Eve and Jason and I wait, for what seems like a very long time, in our rented car parked by the side of the road at the entrance to the suburban development. An older woman is taking care of a toddler in the yard on the corner. She gives us nervous looks, then takes the child into the house. Is there any reason for us to be hopeful about this expedition? I am always hopeful—there *must* be a way to find Alex and Chris.

The sheriff's car comes back. Only Michael's sister and her daughter were in the house. The sheriff searched everywhere, while the sister watched in silence. The attorney thinks it might be possible to subpoena her tomorrow, to ask her what she knows.

We have nothing.

Back at the motel, we plan our return home. We cannot bear to eat in this motel again—last night we were brought eleven packets of pepper but no salt, no silverware, only one salad. Last night it was a joke; tonight the prospect seems unbearably bleak.

Jason and I decide to go and talk to Michael's father, who lives about thirty miles from here. Would we find Michael and the boys there? Is there danger? We call Michael's father first. We cannot imagine doing a pickup without advance surveillance—I feel safer to warn Michael, if he is there. Michael's father says that he will sit up and wait for us.

MONDAY, MAY 10, 11:00 P.M.: We return one rented car, leave Eve to get us a motel room near the airport and to order something for dinner, and Jason and I drive on to see the father. The old man has been drinking while he waits for us. He is gracious as he greets us, then says, "Michael and you folks have never cared one bit about me!" Jason and I are struck with sorrow—we never meant to hurt this old man. He says that he does not know where Michael is, has had no contact with him at all, has no information to give us. He is choosing his words very carefully, I think trying not to say a falsehood. I am fairly certain that he is in fact receiving all of Michael's mail, including all Michael's office receipts, the only current source of income. There must be some contact between them. But I cannot berate this sad old man.

As we drive away, Jason says, "I can imagine that Michael might be very like his father when he is older. I wish I knew the grandfather better—I think I would like him. I wish what is left of our family could hold together." I feel so sad for all of us. I only asked that the marriage be broken; Michael has insisted on tearing the family apart, as well.

We drive back to the motel. Eve has booked us on a very early flight, direct to Minneapolis. We are too tired to talk.

TUESDAY, MAY 11: Jason, Eve, and I parted in the Minneapolis airport, and after I had kissed them and thanked them and turned away my tears came in a flood. Jason came back to me and asked for a ride to the bus station, so that he could go directly to school and meet with his next class. By then I could not stop the tears. I hadn't meant to put Jason through that display. My car still had the two pillows, the favorite nap blankets, the graham crackers, and the thermos of grape juice. Where could I turn next? Only now could I let myself realize how much I had hoped that we could bring them back with us.

Paul helped me to tie up the loose ends. The Pinkerton's investigators checked the airports but got no information about Michael. The St. Louis attorney reported that the judge ruled that it was not possible to subpoena the sister, since no crime was charged. Alan would file an affidavit about that wild, life-endangering ride that Michael took the boys on at midnight.

I got home at noon, slept for an hour, and went back to my office to see patients.

FRIDAY, MAY 14: Michael has called at my office twice in the last week. He says he will never let me talk to Alex and Chrissy until he can talk on demand to Mary. I suspected that he would react that way. His constant refrain is that everything that is happening is my responsibility, that I caused it all to happen by asking for a divorce. Would I have believed that if I had not taken so much time before to think through my own ready assumption of guilt? How can he believe that he has no responsibility for his own actions?

When Michael called the second time to the office he said that he had contacted the adoption agency from which we got Mary, that he was arranging to "reverse her adoption." It sounds as if he means to have her repossessed like a piece of unpaid-for merchandise. All through his childhood his mother made purchases on which she then couldn't keep up the payments. Is he reliving the disappointments of his childhood? He also said, rather ominously, that he had my will and my "body disposition form" (which I had made out years before, donating my body to medical research), and that he didn't "know what to do with them." What a gruesome set of messages!

A letter has also come, referring to my conversation with his father—obviously those two are in contact:

Anna:

You told my father "Michael will be happier without me." You have no right to speak for me.

I am the only person who can know whether I will be happier without you—I don't believe that is true. It would be better if I did feel that way.

Michael

I grieve for him, wonder that he can still send such a letter, and remain angry. I continue to fight to hold on to this house for the children and me. Michael is demanding from everyone to whom he or we owe money that they seize this house and evict us. I think he might return if he could find Jason, Mary, and me sitting on a street corner, starving and homeless. He wants to be able to say, "You see, you can't make it without me."

I talked to an old friend from medical school last week, a man with whom I went through the dissection of a cadaver and other stresses. I told him what I thought was Michael's vision, that I would collapse in his absence. He said, "Of course, I can't think of anyone about whom that fantasy is more foolish." There are some people who have proposed that I feign a sort of collapse as a ruse to bring Michael home. That seems to me to be as dishonest as the pretense that I would be willing to have a reconciliation. My backbone tells me that this is a struggle as deadly serious as between any two forest animals, only waged with the weaponry of modern society. Should I lie down and play dead to get my children back? I am a poor actress, but also my backbone won't bend in that direction. For once I will stand my ground with Michael.

I am working three twelve-hour stints in the hospital Emergency Room each week to earn extra money. I am paying for three mortgages, all of our household expenses, and the costs of looking for and trying to get the boys. Neither Paul nor I can get a very clear perspective on the tangle of these finances.

We are scheduled into court next week for the final divorce action, the necessary weeks having passed since service by publication and the temporary orders for support, custody, and possession of the house. I am certain that if Michael were divorcing me and I didn't appear in court the matter would just proceed. I have heard many stories of women who got caught in such a trap, even women who were prepared to come to court but were never informed of the hearing date. Paul has sent notice of this hearing date to Michael through his attorney, his office mailing address, his father's address, and through Oscar Larson, the hospital's lawyer who is in contact with Michael. Will Michael come back?

Paul advises me that we have no choice but to divide the property, in Michael's absence, so that he has all the debts and I have all the assets. The joint debts can still all fall to me if he defaults and the creditors choose to sue me. Because I am now the only responsible adult trying to conserve whatever I can for the children, I now have to try to take control of everything. But I hate that solution. It makes me feel that I am acting out Michael's worst vision of me as "greedy." Paul is adamant. He and Tom have talked at length about the most sensible legal strategy at this point. Since Michael's avowed intent is to trash whatever resources we have and to plunge me into debt, I feel that I must follow their advice. Surely Paul is a sensitive man, not vindictive, and he would not put me into that "greedy" stance unnecessarily.

Beth has said that she will come to court with me. Her husband always carries a loaded gun to his white-collar job and is as suspicious/angry as Michael; Beth has been a model through whom I have tried to understand Michael. She says that she will make a decision about divorcing her husband after she sees whether I get shot in my effort!

When I think of the possibility that Michael will alight somewhere and take a job, for instance as an Emergency Room doctor, I wonder if anyone will think him odd in his evident anger. And then I think they will just say, "So what, just one more angry doctor." It seems to me that I know many men who are chronically angry, suspicious, and believe that others are out to get them, that none of their troubles are their own doing. Is it the conditions of their competitive work, their longing for a loving mother, or still other common male experiences that contribute to this mental status? Maybe angry paranoia is primarily a male disease. Certainly women may be fearfully paranoid but they are not nearly so likely to be angrily paranoid. We women have been quite well socialized out of even justified angers.

I remember a paper that proposed that the root of all human communication was not the male-hunter bond—one common theory—but the mother-infant bond. Hunters, it was argued, would not have caught very much if they had done a lot of verbal communication. Mothers, on the other hand, have always had to communicate constantly with their young children as a central aspect of interaction and in fact have had to teach their children to communicate. Is there some relationship between chronic male anger and their blocked opportunities to communicate, especially to communicate about feelings?

I hope that my sons will be able to escape the stereotypes of maleness that are so crippling. In many ways it is easier to rear daughters right now. The changes that women are making in their own lives, with the support of other women, are clear in their direction even if they are opposed by strong social forces.

Young men, on the other hand, are inevitably drawn to the side of the strong social forces that resist these changes. Men have not yet begun to create a strong and clearly delineated alternative to woman-using patriarchy. I am certain that they must do that for themselves; any script that requires that women teach humanity to men will fail.

I hear from Clarence, Michael's local doctor-acquaintance, and from friends in Chicago who have had second-hand information about Michael, that he is now talking like the most extreme of woman-haters. There is a surgeon acquaintance of Michael's in Minneapolis, one who always carries a loaded gun, who says that he offered to Michael to come up here and "take care of that broad!"—presumably by gunshot. Michael is said to have replied that he had other ways of taking care of me. It is disquieting to know that there is someone out there who holds so much malevolence toward me, and that he can gain support from like-thinking men whose potential for violence is considerable.

THURSDAY, MAY 20: I have heard of two psychics nearby who are said to be helpful in situations like this. One is in a small town in Wisconsin, and is said to be very good at finding lost things and people. I have called her and find that she has a very elaborate system of making appointments and that she is very busy. I am a little intimidated. There is another psychic in Duluth who has the same name as I. I find it impossible not to hope that she can help. She also is very busy but can see me in two weeks.

Our day in court, the scheduled final divorce, came and went. The judge heard the story from Paul and listened to my testimony. Neither Michael nor his attorney was there, to no one's surprise. The judge decided in the end that Michael should be given another chance to appear, and that he would hear the matter "for the second and final time" in three weeks, to allow Michael to make his claim in the tangled mess of money and property division. Would I have been given that second chance if I had failed to appear?

Mother's Day is coming. I feel an enormous sadness, out of proportion to any feeling that I have ever had about that day and its conventional meaning. Sometime we must have a real mother's day, a women's day, in which we can celebrate all of the pain and joy and grief and ecstasy of mothering.

MONDAY, MAY 24: Jason just called. His roommate saw Michael and Alex and Chris—or so he thought—walking in the streets of Minneapolis, near the university. Michael once had an office in that neighborhood—it is like him to go back to old familiar territory.

Again, I cannot deny my own intense response. If they can be found, if there is the merest chance, we must search and then try to rescue them. I call Kenniston and we work out every contact, every accustomed haunt, that I can think of in Minneapolis. A medical student friend suggests that an acquaintance of hers, a graduate student, might watch or even visit at the home of the surgeon who carries a gun, the single contact-person/place that I think would most draw Michael. Then we remember about the gun and decide not to risk another life. I call Kenniston back and tell him about the possibility of a gun at that place of surveillance.

I have called several friends in Minneapolis to ask if they would be willing to go with me, to help fetch the boys if they can be located. Some are willing and ready—even when I explain the possibility of danger—and others seem comfortable saying that they would not be good at that sort of thing. One close friend is ambivalent, torn: "I would like to think that I would do anything for you, but I cannot say yes to this. I cannot even say why that is, except that it is not a thing that I can bring myself to do."

I calculate that we need to have two people—I being one—to physically pick up the two boys and bring them to a car. There must be someone to drive the car and probably two people—men or strong women who know something about self-defense—to distract or restrain Michael. If there were others willing to help, there are the possibilities of changing cars, phoning the police to say that the children are all right after they have been picked up, calling our home to say that the little boys are safe, staying with or following Michael to see that he does not follow us, and so on. Again, I vacillate between thinking that I must think ahead to and plan for every eventuality and thinking that there is a point at which excessive preplanning will decrease our ability to be flexible, sensible, and creative at moments of decision. My own habits of compulsive attention to detail drive me to plan and plan.

I have terrible difficulties envisioning that actual moment of pickup. It seems to me that if Michael, seeing me, simply lifted Chrissy into his arms, our task would become impossible. I despair at the thought of any kind of violence. I am continually asked if Michael is likely to have and to be ready to shoot a gun, and I simply don't know. In the past his violence has always been psychological, verbal, but from his letters and calls now, I know that he is more than a little unhinged from his usual self and I am not sure what he might do in a desperate situation. I am increasingly impressed by the fact that he is willing to be self-destructive and willing to hurt his children in the interest of punishing or coercing me.

I don't want my friends or agents to be hurt, and I don't want my friends or agents to hurt Michael. Most of all I don't want Alexy and Chrissy to be hurt. I believe that the event of a pickup would have a runaway quality to it that might become uncontrollable—that is, the group of us determined to get those little boys might precipitate some kind of violence.

We put together a team of people who are willing to help get the boys if they can be located—there are some extras in cases someone might be busy or unreachable. I keep wondering at the degree to which not only my own pace and history but also those of my friends and acquaintances are foreign to this sort of action. Are there people who would find this a rather ordinary set of events?

In the course of making these phone calls I have talked to other people who will watch for Michael and the boys in the neighborhood where they were seen and will tell others to be on the alert. I think there is now as wide and tight an organization as can be constructed around that one sighting. Are they really nearby? Jason's roommate has only seen Michael once and has only seen Alex and Chris in pictures. Perhaps it is a false alarm.

I have heard a bit of lore in this town that I find curious: it is felt by some at least that Michael has a right of access to Chris because Chris is biologically his child but does not have that same right of access to the adopted children who are seen as belonging only to me. I wonder if that opinion is reflected anywhere in legal thinking? It does make it clear that it is Michael's seed, the line of inheritance, that is the root of the father-right, whereas the mother-right is based on care taking. Little if anything is said about the rights of the children themselves to a safe and predictable world.

What if I said that neither Chris nor Jason was really Michael's seed-child? Who is to know but me? I am struck by the collusion of women—even someone like me who has always been at least potentially self-supporting—in *giving* to a man a legal right to our children. I wonder if I would be able to pretend or invent some other paternity if I needed to, to safeguard Chris.

Meg and Jason and I have each separately thought of a place to look for Michael. Our cabin on the Wisconsin border has a phone. Now that the weather is getting warm enough to make that place comfortable, despite its meager heating system, we should call there at intervals. Ann is making that call every day from work, prepared to ask for a fictitious person and claim a wrong number if Michael should answer. I have also called the neighbors nearby. They are old and don't want to get involved but have promised to watch our cabin for any signs of activity and to call me. They can't understand why I just can't call the police and ask them to find Michael and return the boys. I can't understand, either, even after all these weeks.

Is anything justified for a man who must punish an uppity woman? I feel as well as hear two parallel reactions: that a man's wife, his owned mother/property, has no right to reject him and should in that event be punished; and that to steal her children and run away, especially to leave her with a perplexing tangle of debts, is an appropriate and perhaps even an admirable solution. No one has said any of this to me directly, in so many words. But the tacit approval I hear, even the faint hint of envy at Michael's living out such a wild fantasy, makes me aware of a pressure of opinion to which I can only react with astonishment and horror. And a sense of wonder at myself—I thought that I had understood, could predict, the range and depth of men's abiding anger at women. Why do these reactions still leave me breathless with protest?

When Paul spoke to the FBI agent yesterday, for instance, about acting on the possibly fraudulent letter Michael sent to the bank, the agent said that Michael "would, of course, have a ready defense to the charge because he could say that he was embroiled in a marital dispute." If I had committed a fraudulent act, would I be excused on the grounds that I was having a difficult time with my husband?

The stories I hear about other recent cases of parental kidnaping generally have a similar pattern. The majority of the recent notable cases are kidnapings by fathers. Observers agree that almost always the children are not the central issue but that the chief motive is punishment of the wife. Kidnapings often happen a second and third time. And in many cases after the children return to their mothers and their homes they appear to be seriously traumatized psychologically—fearful, mistrustful, having night terrors, needing special schooling or psychotherapy. There are also some gruesome stories of physical violence—agents who Mace or beat mothers from whom children are stolen; one double death, father and three-year-old son, in a car crash during a chase-to-rescue; and one incident of a father coming back to his two previously kidnaped sons, shooting first the children and then himself.

I wonder if I should somehow swallow my own pain at their loss, in the belief that anything I do to affect Michael's present angry/crazy spirit could further endanger Alex and Chris? The present danger to their lives, their well-being, their minds and souls causes me far greater pain than just my own empty ache for their presence. How could I weigh the good of rescuing them from present danger against the risk of instigating further danger for them? That is my constant dilemma, and no one has the answer to that question. I must in the end believe that there is somehow some "hand of fate" that will guide my decisions, my acts, and their outcome.

My worries about the boys are unbearable precisely because I am primed to act on their behalf, to safeguard them with my very life if necessary, to give every ounce of my strength and will for them—and now, today, there is nothing I can do to protect them against a very real and certain danger. The song says,

> Like a young tree, I see you sway and bend,
> And I'm so afraid, afraid you might break,
> Tossed by the wind, the storms that come your way,
> And careless strangers, seeing fruit, who reach out to take.

FRIDAY, JUNE 4: We have found them again. After the urgent mobilization of ten days ago, which came to naught, I have felt profoundly depressed but also strangely, intuitively hopeful. Ann has called the telephone number at our cabin every day. Jason says, "I think he is nearby. I think he will come to that final day in court (now less than a week away) to get his property. If you listen to what he says, that's what he really wants."

Michael did of course know about the last "final date," because he wrote a letter to the bank immediately after that day, believing that we were divorced. But Jason's hunch corresponds to a strong intuition of mine that we are nearing the end of this thing. Mary dreamed that Michael came back to our house, looking for something, two nights ago.

Today, when Ann made her now routine call to our cabin, Michael answered. She was so startled she nearly lost her composure. But she recovered quickly and said her prepared piece, asking for a nonexistent person and apologizing for dialing a wrong number.

Five minutes later Michael called our office. In an unplanned gaffe that drives me even deeper into compulsive consider-every-contingency preplanning, Ann was the person who answered the telephone. We think it quite likely that Michael may have matched her voice in the two calls, that he may be tipped off to the fact that I know where he is.

But today our machinery is superbly organized. Caught again without a plan, I call Paul to put him on notice, to be ready to make contact with the "underworld type" and to stay available for advice. I call Pinkerton's, by now knowing all of the staff in the Minneapolis office by name; they also know me and the complicated story and clearly communicate their empathy and concern. They will have an agent in the north go immediately to the cabin.

Meg, Barbara, and I will drive to the cabin. We need a fourth person, so Barbara calls a friend of hers, a patient in our office. Elaine, like most people in this town, has had very little accurate information about the kidnaping—like others, for instance, she has wondered if I was unable to have the custody of the boys through the courts, puzzled that I had not simply found them and brought them back. Barbara fills her in on the story very briefly by telephone, and she agrees to come out of friendship for Barbara and perhaps partly out of curiosity. I am very grateful for her willingness and a little uncomfortable, since I do not know her very well.

Ann will stay here this time. She will go with her own children to my house, to be with Mary and to woman the telephone as our central telephone contact. She will keep Paul posted on developments and will notify Jo (my friend with the vacation cabin) that the boys and I may be arriving soon.

Within an hour of Ann's call to Michael the Pinkerton's investigators are said to be on their way to the cabin. We have canceled all patients in the office except the three with acute illnesses, and they have come in and been seen. Meg has gathered for us a collection of sweaters and jackets, apples and raisins, bought Mary a present to take to a birthday party this afternoon, got money at the bank. Elaine has arrived with her own collection of snack food and a full tank of gas. We are ready to leave.

FRIDAY, JUNE 4, MIDNIGHT: A tension of uncertainty—have they slipped away from us again?

On the way to the cabin we four stopped to rent a car—only one this time, to be exchanged for Elaine's car if we need to make a switch—and to call Ann. She reported that a Lieutenant Anderson and two other Pinkerton's investigators were at the cabin at 1:00 P.M. and that the cabin was empty. There were recent tire tracks, new since last night's rain. They are watching the cabin and will meet us in front of the library in the nearby town at our estimated time of arrival.

We arrive at the libary in our two cars a half-hour before meeting time. Elaine hides her car behind the town bank. We wait, sitting on the lawn of the library, my back to the road in case Michael should drive by. As before, we are dressed for outside running.

A shabby old car drives up and parks behind our rented car. Two old, grizzled, and rather dirty woodsmen get out. They glance at us and we glance uncertainly at them. Meg, who has a mental picture of short-haired and rather nattily dressed detectives, whispers "Could they be?" We all watch each other warily for a few minutes. I suppose if they are looking for Dr. Demeter I don't exactly look my part, either. We say simultaneously "Lieutenant Anderson?" and "Dr. Demeter?" each with an expression of relief.

A third man has joined the search—"Three for the price of two," says Lieutenant Anderson—and he is presently watching the cabin. They ask if I have brought pictures of Michael and the boys, for as they were arriving they saw a large white camper-van driving down the road just past the cabin. They look at the pictures that I have and nod sagely—they *think* that the driver of the camper-van might have been Michael. They did not see the boys and do not even have a very good description of the van itself. They did not notice the license. I cannot guess what kind of vehicle Michael might now be driving, after having wrecked his own car in St. Louis.

We talk about possibilities. If Michael has just taken the boys out for a drive or to go shopping, he may come back any time but would probably be back by ten or so. (Does he schedule his day at all in accordance with the needs of two little boys?) We agree to meet at the cabin at 10:00. If they have not returned we will go in the cabin and see what information we can find.

We separate and the four of us women go to find some dinner. There is a new restaurant in the little town, an Italian/vegetarian restaurant, and we have a dinner worthy of a festive occasion, complete with wine. Our mood is an eerie mixture of fear, excitement, apprehension, hope, high energy.

As we approach the cabin we are startled to see an old car with no lights on traveling slowly past the cabin. It is one of Lieutenant Anderson's men. Meg and I go with Lieutenant Anderson into the cabin.

It is very difficult to get any clear picture of the place without lights. We still think that their return is possible and don't want to frighten Michael away by turning on lights. We search with flashlights. There are three plates with spaghetti, still wet—the stain of spaghetti sauce for Michael and Alex, plain spaghetti without sauce for Chrissy. Is it my imagination, or is the pot of coffee on the stove still faintly warm? Otherwise, remarkably little —no children's toys, no odd scraps of children's clothes. Did he make a careful effort, before they left, to remove all traces of themselves? How would he have explained that to the children?

There are Minneapolis newspapers for the entire month of May. It would seem that Michael came to Minneapolis soon after the St. Louis search—so perhaps Jason's roommate really did see them. It seems strange and awesome that we in the house had such strong intuitive feelings about their nearness in the past few weeks.

There is little more to be done tonight. I want to get out of the cabin, hoping (against hope) that they will come back tonight. Anderson and his colleagues will watch the cabin during the night, and we agree to meet here again in the morning.

We have found rooms in a quaint and lovely lodge. This trip is an odd alternation of excitement, fear, and luxurious relaxation. I have not had any vacation for so long—I wish that I could relax and enjoy the nice bits of this weekend.

SATURDAY, JUNE 5, 5:00 P.M.: We are back home, empty-handed again.

Meg, Barbara, Elaine, and I searched the cabin again early this morning. We thought that we had lost contact with Anderson and his men, but we learned later that they had observed us the whole time from the woods. It was a little unnerving to know that we had been watched unawares.

In daylight we did find one very important piece of information, after sifting through virtually everything in the cabin. In one of the trash baskets we found an envelope from the automobile registration bureau in Wisconsin, with a license number printed on the outside. From that we may be able to find out what kind of car he is now driving. There was fresh and recently purchased food in the refrigerator—perhaps they really are planning to come back to the cabin. Or perhaps the telephone call frightened Michael away—I wonder if I shall ever know.

Anderson brushed the drive so that he can identify new tire tracks. He will get in touch with the automobile registration bureau in Wisconsin and will try to find out what kind of car is registered to that license number. He and his colleagues are elaborate in their generosity and courtesy—we four women have all believed from the moment that we met these Pinkerton's investigators that they would not hesitate to help us rescue the boys, if they could be located. Here, at least, that "underworld type" would not be needed.

Anderson answers all of my thanks by saying that he would "do anything for those two poor little boys." Here, again, that rarity, a man who is genuinely concerned about the children. In fact, both Anderson and the other investigator that we met here—both men past sixty—have been courteous and straightforward with us, neither doubting our determination and competence to do what we came to do nor communicating innuendoes about marriage or any other between-sex relationship. I wonder if their attitudes toward us and their focus on the fate of the boys is not a function of their age: they are past the time of life in which sexual exploitation is a driving preoccupation. For me their directness is refreshing; if all of the offices and agencies to which I have applied for help in the past three months were staffed with Lieutenant Andersons, I have no doubt that the boys would be home by now.

Anderson says that he has contacted friends in the Wisconsin state police and arranged for surveillance for both the camper-van and for the license number we found, FOE 120. They have been told that Michael has a dying relative and would be alarmed by any direct conversation with the police—Anderson will be notified immediately if either vehicle is spotted.

The trip home was quiet. We four were sad, tired, wrung out. I have probably incurred another $1,000 of Pinkerton's charges —I wonder how many times I will be able to make this kind of response to a sighting of Michael, and if we will succeed in rescuing the boys before all of my savings are used. Barbara tells me as we part, back home, that Elaine was overwhelmed and a little frightened at the intensity of our shared experience.

Tonight I cry and cry, a communion with myself that I do not want anyone to share or to interrupt. Will we ever find them, bring them home? Can he really stay hidden forever? Could he find work, keep moving, change names, go to another country? What must it mean to Alexy and Chrissy to have to leave their own vacation cabin, taking everything that they brought, leaving no trace of themselves behind? Do they still remember me? Do they still believe that I love them? Do they feel bereft of me as I feel of them?

TUESDAY, JUNE 15: Another clue, another place to look. The dean of our medical school in Cleveland called me this morning to say that Michael had just called him. I had been in touch with the dean, an old and trusted friend. One of Michael's friends from Navy days works at the university where Michael and I attended medical school, and the dean had asked him to urge Michael to call, if they had any contact. The dean this morning urged Michael himself to come to his office and talk. Michael said that he might do that.

The dean has arranged through the university switchboard to have his own office telephone tapped, so that Michael can be located if he ever calls that office again. This is the first time in the whole fifteen weeks of this ordeal that a phone tap has been arranged—through the combined powers of a male in authority and a large institution.

I myself called Michael's friend. Michael did visit him, two days ago. He said that both boys looked fearful, withdrawn, depressed, and very dirty and unkempt. He says that he does not know where Michael is now, but I am not sure that he would tell me if he knew. I sense that they are not at that friend's house now.

Michael's friend says that Michael is doing a terrible thing, both self-destructive and harmful to the little boys. I think he convinced himself of that as he talked to me, as he heard himself describe Alex and Chris to me. He says that if Michael comes back to his house he will try to talk Michael into leaving Alex and Chrissy with him. But he would not, apparently, notify me that the boys were there.

I put down the telephone, astonished. The old male trip: when in doubt, take over. Michael's friend has apparently made a judgment of me and my capacity to mother Alex and Chris solely on the basis of Michael's ravings. He would choose to allow his wife to take care of those boys rather than allow them to go to their own mother. "Careless strangers, seeing fruit, who reach out to take."

I have contacts in Cleveland from my days as a student. Through a chain of personal connections Paul is able to talk to a seasoned officer in the Family Division of the city police force. He tells Paul that there is, of course, nothing that can be done officially, but that he will request that the city patrolmen watch for Michael's car, which we presume to be the green 1968 four-door Chevrolet registered to Wisconsin plate FOE 120. Once more I contact Pinkerton's, now to ask for surveillance on the house of Michael's Navy friend and on the house of one mutual friend from medical school days. I also make contact, with the help of an old and close friend of mine, with an attorney who knows about the complexities of child-snatching cases.

Meg says, "If Michael's not in Cleveland you had better find a way to lure him there—you and your children have better protection there than in any state you've contacted so far!"

FRIDAY, JUNE 18: I fear that the trace to Cleveland was another false alarm. I had gone so far as to arrange a search-and-rescue party, several friends who said they would be willing to go with me. I am as astounded at the generosity of the many folk who are willing to help as I am shaken that all official legal channels seem to be closed. The IRS has ruled that I am to be held responsible for Michael's unpaid income tax. And the loan from the bank that Michael got at the time of our move is in my name as well.

Michael has said, I understand, that the hospital must choose between him and me. Since he is a cardiologist his monetary value to the hospital is much the greater; a major goal for my family practice is to keep patients out of the hospital, both through preventive health care and by implementing home care for illness whenever possible. I begin to have serious doubts that I will be able to remain in this town and practice medicine.

I have learned that in order for the hospital to be accredited (which it must be in order to be able to collect Medicare/Medicaid funds) there will be a physician committee to assess the mental and physical competence of all physician staff members. Ironically, I am appointed to that committee for the next year. I could not approve Michael as a physician who is trustworthy and of good judgment. From what I know of his present state, I don't think that he is safe with patients. I would, of course, have to absent myself from the committee's deliberations when Michael's case was being considered.

Clarence, who continues to be in touch with Michael by telephone, tells me that Michael now says he will get temporary licenses to practice, work in one location for a brief time, and then move on to another state. I know by now that Clarence only reports to me when he has something alarming to predict or report. Nonetheless I panic again; I had always assumed that Michael would run out of money as he used up all of his collections from accounts receivable, and would then be forced to come back or at least to reveal himself by applying through the medical boards of registration of Minnesota and Ohio. Now I learn by talking to officials at the AMA that he can indeed get temporary licenses in several states through rather casual procedures and can practice for weeks or months before it is discovered that he has not applied for regular licensure. Perhaps he really could find a way to remain a fugitive for months or years, as he has threatened all along.

I have thought so many times (and talked to Paul) about negotiating some sort of compromise with Michael, in return for the children. I really do believe that Michael would trade the children for money, property, an absolution from all debt, or something of the sort. I could only file bankruptcy if that were to happen. And Paul is adamant in his advice; he feels that Michael is so completely irrational that any effort to compromise would be futile, that Michael will not rest until he has everything he wants. "And," says Paul, "what he wants is you."

Clarence said, when we talked the other day, "You know, he really does love you."

I held my head in despair and exasperation. "Clarence, do you know what he has said and done to me in the past months? And what he has done to Chris and Alex in an effort to get to me? Love like that I can do without."

Clarence said, "No, you don't understand. He really does love you. He says if you will take him back he will stand up in this town and say that everything he has been saying about you is a lie."

How can these men comprehend a love that has been used to hurt so badly? Do they not understand that there are watershed points in a relationship, points past which you can't go back? Does Michael think that by beating me bloody he can reduce me to a point where I say, "All right, I'll be your wife again"?

I talk to Jason about this. Jason says, "Be his wife? In a cage? Would he plant grass and trees around the cage so that he could pretend that he was taking good care of you?"

My own grief, this past week, has focused on Chrissy's birthday. When I was a child I never realized how much a birthday is a mother's day. When my children have birthdays I always celebrate not only the child but also the birthing. Reliving the hours of Chrissy's birth this year was a ritual of intense recall and a sense of sharing with all women whose children are taken away, however that might happen. "Child of my body, bone of my bone, apple of my eye."

FRIDAY, JULY 2: Clarence is actively working as a go-between now, talking to Michael by telephone almost every day. I still think that Michael must be running out of money. I have said that I will not negotiate with Michael about the terms of the divorce until Alex and Chrissy have been returned, but that when that has happened I will negotiate about everything. Paul, who is deeply and ethically opposed to bankruptcy, argues that if I were to put myself in that position I would severely limit my ability to work as a physician and to support my children. I am torn, desperate.

If Clarence can arrange for me to meet with Michael, I plan to agree. I would not hesitate to use that meeting as an opportunity to take the boys away with me. Clarence has suggested a restaurant in a town just over the state line into Wisconsin— Michael is adamant that he will not come into this state, apparently believing that the police here are looking for him. I work out another complicated plan to use the help of several friends in wresting the boys from Michael. I even drive to that restaurant, thinking about where we each would sit, how many cars we would need, and on and on.

Michael called Janet, who had sat with me that day when I told him that I must have a divorce. He proposed that he might come back if he could believe he would have custody of the children, and they would spend half their time with him and half their time with me. Janet asked how, if he were convinced that I was such a bad mother, he could think of letting me be with the children half the time. He said, "Oh, it would be all right because I would live very nearby and could supervise everything she does."

That solution sounds as much like a nondivorce divorce as I

can possibly imagine. I am increasingly certain that Michael
simply cannot deal with the idea of divorce. The whole set of
issues that I hoped that Michael could begin to resolve in his
own mind, and in his life, by consulting with the divorce counselors is still a central source of confusion and distress for him.
I wonder if it might have been easier for him if I had said that
I am in love with another man whom I wanted to marry. Would
that be more tolerable for Michael—and perhaps also for public
opinion in this town? Is the notion that I simply don't want to
live with him any more, would prefer to be an unmarried mother,
a cause for perplexity and perhaps extreme anger because of the
implied challenge to institutionalized ownership of women and
children by men? I can of course earn a living and I have always
done the lioness's share of child care and housework. It is astonishing to me that anyone could suppose that I could not manage
for myself and my children, that my children and I must belong
to someone.

Two days ago I went to visit the psychic in Duluth—the one
whose name (also by marriage) is the same as mine. I was there
for nearly two hours, for a charge of $20. When I arrived, before
she started to talk, she knew almost nothing about the problem
except that Michael had run away with the two little boys and
had been gone with them for sixteen weeks. The suggestions
that she made were fascinating. Some of what she said confimed
what I already knew, but there was much that I will want to
try to confirm later.

She did some automatic writing, thought that she was hearing
first from a woman who was disgusted with Michael (his mother,
dead nine years?) and then from a younger man, a take-charge
person (whom I could only imagine to be Michael's mother's
younger brother, a young man regarded by his family as of promise, who died at an early age). The latter said that Michael had
wanted to go to Canada but he had prevented him. (It apparently was true that Michael had thought about going to Canada
to escape responsibility for the IRS debt.)

The same source said that Michael was capable of violence

toward me, most likely by gunfire, but that he (the automatic writing source) would try to protect me, perhaps by causing a misfire or deflecting Michael's hand. (I hope not to have to learn whether that prediction is true.)

She used cards to clue her description of the present and recent past, noting, for instance that one of the children had lost or torn a shoe and that Michael had just bought him a new pair of shoes. (This was true for Alex, as he later told me.)

She said that they were now or had recently been in Seattle and had for the most part been traveling along coasts, that Michael "must always be near water." (Clarence later told me that Michael had called him during that week from Seattle, and the boys often described their "trip" as being always near the ocean.)

She said that he may come back soon "to take care of his money" (meaning, perhaps, that he will return for the postponed day of the final divorce decree, scheduled for next week) and that he is traveling very hard right now on back roads, afraid that the police everywhere are looking for him.

She said that the boys are still alive—the single most comforting thing she told me.

She said that the boys would, later on, regard their "trip" as an adventure, a special and good bond between them. In the weeks and months ahead I held on to that prediction, wanting very much to believe that they were constructed of a strong enough psychological sturdiness to be able to use these months to some good purpose, that the effect would not just be devastatingly harmful to them.

She concluded that because Michael is clearly (to her understanding) in an irrational state, his actions in the future are very hard to predict. She could only say some of the things she thought Michael might do and could not weigh probabilities—she said that he is essentially planless or, more accurately, the victim of his own shifting plans.

I am impressed by the information given to me by the other Anna Demeter—a plain, middle-aged housewife sitting in the kitchen of her small house in a working-class neighborhood. I want to believe much of what she has told me. In that respect, I am little different from the patient who begins to heal herself by using what her doctor has told her.

I talked this morning to the wife of Michael's Navy friend in Cleveland. I asked if it were true, as her husband said, that they would simply keep the two boys and would not notify me. She was startled at the suggestion and said that she would not allow that to happen, whatever her husband wished. She took my telephone number and promised to call me if they had any more contact with Michael. She was even more disturbed than her husband about the appearance and behavior of Alexy and Chrissy. The pain in my heart is palpable—how can I, their mother, defend them, care for them, protect them? What can I do? [As I write this there is a short documentary on TV about child snatching. The TV camera follows as a young father takes his small boy out of the child's own yard, away from his mother. The face of the little boy is bereft, lost, inutterably sad as he and his father, fugitives, take themselves to a place where they cannot be found. The father is asked by a TV commentator, "It seems as if the kidnaped children are the real victims of these tragedies. What do you suppose it means to your little boy to be taken away in this fashion?"

The father replies, "I thought about that a lot last night. I decided it doesn't mean nothin' to him."]

There have been so many times in the last months when someone has told me that they had heard that Michael was coming back soon. Now Clarence thinks again that might be so, Janet thinks that Michael might be planning to come back, and the other Anna Demeter says that even though Michael is not in control of his plans he will be strongly drawn to come back "to take care of his money." The hearing in court is only four days away.

On my way home from the office tonight I see Clarence on the street and stop my car to give him a message about a patient. He says, as an afterthought, "Oh, by the way, Michael called last night and said that he is coming back to appear in court on Tuesday. He says that he is now sure he can take the children away from you by legal means."

I was menstruating when the boys disappeared. I have had only one more menses in the four months since they have been lost. Now, within a half hour of this conversation with Clarence, I am bleeding again. I know that *I* believe the boys will be back very soon.

SATURDAY, JULY 3: Just at the end of my office hours this morning, as I am packing my equipment to go home, I am called to see a patient in the Emergency Room, a child with an earache.

As I drive into the Emergency Room parking area, I glance at the last car in the parking line—I have become a compulsive reader of license plate numbers, especially noticing Wisconsin plates. I read off the letters and numbers, and suddenly my attention jumps. F . . . O . . . E . . . 120, my pulse races. It is that car!

I pull my car close to the Emergency Room entrance, away from Michael's car. Clarence comes out of the Emergency Room door. I point numbly to Michael's car and Clarence says, "Yes, they are here." My mind is spinning—will I be able to see the boys, touch them, take them home with me?

There are a lot of people standing around in the Emergency Room. I feel dazed and disoriented—afterward many people told me that they had been there, yet I had not known they were there. I cannot see Michael or Alex or Chrissy. Clarence tells me that they are waiting in the conference room.

As Clarence and I walk toward the conference room Michael and Chris, and then Alex following after, appear at the end of the corridor. The boys run to me, shrieking with surprise and delight, "Mommy! Mommy!" They rush toward me, I take a few steps in their direction, and then stoop down to receive their hurtling bodies, one in each arm. They press in close, hold me tightly with their arms, and say nothing. My eyes are filled with tears.

I try to scoop them up, to carry them out the door to my car, but they are too heavy, too gangly. We walk, each child holding one of my hands. We go to my car, get in, and lock the doors. I say, "I am so glad that I found you. We are going home now."

Someone else will have to see the child with the earache.

KEEPING

SUNDAY, JULY 4: Alex and Chrissy are terribly thin, although I think they have grown taller. Their ribs stick out alarmingly. Both are rather quiet, rather apprehensive. They seem to have lost much of their trusting spontaneity.

Since we came back to the house yesterday, to a tearful and joyous reunion with Jason, Mary, Meg, and her daughter Molly, we have all tried to give Chris and Alexy room to rediscover us and their home. After four months of being told that what they had always known—home and mommy—was now not good for them, I am sure their return here is not entirely easy.

Chrissy took my face in his hands yesterday and said, "I really *do* like you, Mommy!" Later, when he was sitting on his bed staring into space, I reached out my arms to hold him and he flinched back.

Alex, even more than Chris, plays wordlessly with his toys, talks almost not at all. Once yesterday when I was sitting next to him he said, "Every time I told my daddy that I wanted to go back to my mommy he just shouted 'No!' "

We have let both of them play in silence, when that seemed to be what they wanted. Mary, especially, has a nice instinct about them and sits beside one or both of them just close enough to touch. Each of the boys keeps coming to sit on my lap, content to be held and to listen to my old lullabies.

Apparently they did not know that they were going to see me, to come home with me. A friend who is a nurse called to say that she had been in the Emergency Room when we were reunited, and that she and others had cried to see us. She said that she had seen Michael walking up and down the corridors with the boys. Alex had asked, "Why are we staying here so long?"

Michael had answered crossly, "We have to wait for somebody; too bad it's taking so long."

Either Michael did not intend to return them to me and was persuaded to by folks at the hospital or, in his usual fashion with children, he had not told them what was going to happen. Chrissy said, "Our Daddy brought us to that hospital, and then Mommy *found* us there." It is as if, because Michael did not tell them what was about to happen, he gets no credit from them for having brought them back to me.

Chrissy woke up five times in the night, crying "Mommy." Each time he was never really awake, but was comforted by stroking and holding and my quiet voice. And yet in his waking times he calls both Meg and me "Mommy," and is content if either of us answers. I suppose, once disconnected from the validity of the only mommy he knew, told that that connection was no good and that there would be another mommy or mommies, he has learned to accept any giving adult female as a possible mommy. It pains me to hear him address Meg that way and accept her response.

We must get out of this house. I feel as if we are barricaded. I do not dare let even Mary, much less Alex or Chris, out of doors. None of us is accustomed to living that way in this house. The children don't understand why they can't go in and out of un-locked doors, as we have always done, why they can't play in the garden. I cannot bring myself to tell them they might be stolen again, that their father is unpredictable, cruel, perhaps really crazy, a danger to them. We are prisoners.

Tomorrow we will go to Jo's cabin. For all the weeks that the boys were gone we planned to go there with them when or if we could find and rescue them. Jo has kept a suitcase full of their clothes and books and toys, ready for that hoped-for day. Jo, who has four grown children and runs a day-care center, has been like an older sister to me throughout all this trouble.

Tuesday is the scheduled day for the final divorce action in court. On the last day in court the judge heard all preliminary information; what happens next Tuesday should be only a hearing on property division, a judicial decision, and then a formal signing to the end of the marriage. I suspect, however, that a postponement will be asked and granted, and that we have only come to the beginning of the legal struggles toward a divorce.

Chrissy has awakened three times in the four hours since I put him to bed, crying again. When I go to him and hold him, he seems lost—his crying becomes a call for "Mommy."

MONDAY, JULY 5: Alex, Chris, Mary, and I have moved to Jo's cabin for a week. Barbara has canceled my patient appointments in the office, explaining that I am taking a week of vacation. I will drive back to town on three nights to stay overnight in my house and work my twelve-hour Emergency Room stints at the hospital—I do not want it to be thought that *I* have now run away.

Jason, who is working at a drugstore for the summer, will come up here on his two days off. Meg and Molly are also planning to visit off and on.

Before we left to drive here I stopped at my office with the boys. Alex had been in the office as a patient shortly before he went away, so we had a record of his height and weight. In the four months that he was gone he grew an inch and a half and lost two and a half pounds—a not inconsiderable loss, since he was slim to start with. That pattern of continued growth in stature and loss of weight is typical of emotionally deprived children. Chris seems to have done the same, but I do not have a "before" record of his height and weight.

The boys' eating patterns in the last three days remind me of the behavior of severely disturbed children. However, their improvements are very rapid as one might expect of basically healthy children. On Saturday they refused to sit at table with the family, refused to eat anything that was offered as a meal; I simply fed them whatever I could induce them to ask for (ice cream and toast), and in fact they ate almost nothing. Yesterday, Sunday, they ate a little more but still nothing like an ordinary day's quota; they sat at the table but only on my lap or Jason's, Meg's, or Jo's. Today they are eating better still, but only of the special things they request, and they are asking to be fed. They are pacing each other in this, imitating each other alternatively. It is as if they were recapitulating some infant-to-child sequence of holding/spoon-feeding/self-feeding, much as a disturbed or traumatized child regresses to infantile stages and then responds to comforting guidance back to the age-appropriate level. Between the boys and me there is much silent lap sitting and holding.

We have asked them few questions about their being away, letting them talk when they want. They tell of some of the things they did and saw, but speak little about Michael. Neither has asked to see him or even asked where he is. I have told them that they will see him someday soon (thinking that they might be anxious about losing him) but neither seems to feel urgent about being with him.

I have told them how sad I was when they were gone, and how hard we all looked to find them. Chrissy, especially, has seemed to find pleasure in the idea that we all were looking for them; he asked me to name all the people who were looking. He said to me, "And when I was gone did you cry and cry?"

I said, "I certainly did, 'cause I missed you so much. How did you know that I was crying?"

Chrissy snuggled into my shoulder. "Because I was crying too."

Meg and Jason and Jo are worried about my physical safety when I am in town and working at the Emergency Room. The parking lot at the hospital is ill lit at night, and my heart pounds as I go to and from my car. Clarence stops me in the hospital corridor and urges me to have someone with me, for my protection against Michael. I have decided not to do that, for reasons that are impossible to explain to Clarence and difficult to say even to Meg and Jo.

The threat that I continue to hear is that Michael might shoot me with a gun. It seems to me that if he were determined to do that, no bodyguard would be able to protect me. On the other hand, I feel pressed by the situation to admit that, in fact, a woman alone cannot exist in security and safety. It feels as if I am being told that even if I can survive the theft of my children and the disaster of financial ruin I cannot, in the end, survive (without male protection) an incident of violent attack. Clarence, at least, seems to be saying that if I will not have Michael then I must ask for protection from another man, and that situations can endlessly be contrived (for instance, threat of gunshot) that will require me to seek protection.

I will live this out on my own wit and strength. It is such an unreal situation that I have few guidelines to confirm my own sense of reason and rationality. I am careful to see that I am not followed and try to keep a cool head with my pulse racing.

WEDNESDAY, JULY 7: We are not yet divorced. Oscar Larson came to court yesterday, representing Michael. (I asked Paul if that were not a conflict of interest, since Oscar is attorney for the hospital. Paul only shrugged and said that it was strange.) Oscar told the judge that he should leniently allow another postponement on the grounds that Michael needs to find legal counsel and prepare for the case. I wonder, again, if I would have been dealt with so forgivingly had I done what Michael has done. The postponement is indefinite.

Chrissy continues to cry out in the night. Alex said that when those three stopped in motels he, Alex, slept alone in one big bed while Chris and Michael slept together in the other bed—an arrangement that made Alex feel excluded. But it is Chrissy who is disturbed in the night; every night he ends up in my bed, needing the security of an adult body to hold onto.

Jo is impressed at their steadily increasing spontaneity and appearance of security. She knew them before they went away, of course, and was saddened by their tight, pinched, expressionless faces when we first came up here five days ago. Now they play with some abandon and approach the adults and Jason and Mary with the appearance of trust. They only rarely ask now to be fed.

Michael came to where Jason works yesterday and, as Jason says, "talked at me." After all those weeks of separation, there was no conversation about how Jason had been or what he was doing in his life now. Only a harangue from Michael about the necessity of taking the boys away from me because I was so neglectful.

Jason is openly angry at Michael about the little boys' appearance and behavior. I am sure the excesses of Jason's eighteen-year-old anger reflect his disappointment about the events following Michael's return. I think that Jason had wanted to believe that one day Michael would come back and begin to act reasonable and responsible, would somehow agree that what he had been doing was not good for anyone. Jason was not prepared for Michael's continued self-justification and preoccupation with his own angry schemes.

I am concerned about returning home at the end of the week and exposing Mary to Michael's ravings. At twelve, she will be even more vulnerable than Jason to his raging anger at me and his accusations that I am a bad mother. I must, of course, return to work, and Mary cannot be a prisoner in the house. There must be some solution.

SUNDAY, JULY 11: We are settled in for a siege. Paul expects that working through the terms of the divorce will be a matter of days or even weeks. He advises extreme caution, both for fear of a rekidnaping of the boys and for my own safety.

I have thought about taking us all far away. Jo, especially, has urged me to stay at home, primarily because of the need for Paul and me to work closely to bring the divorce to an end.

Mary has gone to the summer camp run by Jo's son. During our week at the cabin Mary had a chance to meet several of the counselors from that camp who visited at Jo's cabin, and she herself asked if she could go to the camp. I am content with that solution; she was happy when I drove her to camp today, and it gives her a respite from Michael's harassments.

Alex and Chrissy will stay during the day at Jo's day-care center. The center has had previous experience with children at risk of kidnaping and has a protocol for that sort of danger. In Jo's experience, the risk of another attempt at kidnaping is significant. I am fortunate to have her wisdom. In addition, and more important, it is an excellent day-care center, a healing place for Alex and Chris. For now, I think, it is important that the two boys stay together because I think the presence of each is reassuring to the other. There has developed, however, since they went away, a strong and tense competition between them. It will be good for them to be at the same center but in different rooms and with different adults to take care of them.

Through the last week they became much less apprehensive about my physical presence. At first they wanted constantly to have me in their sight, wanted only me to help them with dressing and toileting and play. Before they went away they were both very self-confident children, at ease with almost everyone, and some of those old habits are coming back. But having spent four months with a single adult, one crazed with anger and confusion, the boys will need a great deal of reassurance that they can predict what will happen to them from one day to the next, and that there are lots of people around who can and will love and help them. Most of all they need to know that I am here for both of them, predictably, calmly, and equitably.

I am enormously grateful for the help of Jo and Meg and Jason and Mary. My own worries about the divorce, about what will happen to my practice and the possibility of a need to move, the threat of great indebtedness, and the suggestion of my own personal danger, limit my ability to be what the boys need, an endlessly available, endlessly even-handed, endlessly reassuring mother. Even at my best and most resourceful, I am not sure that I could be enough for them right now.

It has been, on the whole, a very good week. Jason and Mary have been marvelous with Alexy and Chrissy. I feel among us a new sense of allegiance, a new knitting together of a strong family. The concern of all of us for the welfare of each is palpable. We focus on mealtimes, on putting to bed and getting up again, on helping each other. We are growing stronger in peaceability and caring.

SATURDAY, JULY 17: The divorce has slowed to a seemingly endless postponement. I understand from Paul that Michael is determined to challenge my custody of the children in court, and that both Paul and Oscar Larson are working hard to discourage him from doing that. In part they are protecting their reputation as attorneys, since judges hate to be asked to decide custody issues and would very much prefer that such matters were settled out of court. For now, no one can push Michael off his intention.

Alex and Chris are getting better daily. They say remarkably little about Michael. Chris said to Jo, "We went away for a long time and we were all by ourselves. Now our daddy is all by himself." I think, or at least hope, that they feel they have permission to talk freely about him, for they tell many stories about things they did during those four months. It is only as if he as a person is unimportant to them right now, or else the cause of some tension and pain. They have not once asked to see him.

Michael has ordered Oscar to ask the judge for visitation rights with the little boys. Paul says again what he has said so many times, "No judge will deny a father the right to see his children." But Paul also is apprehensive about the children's safety, both physical and psychological. He will ask the judge to limit visitation, to arrange some sort of safeguard so that at least there could not easily be another kidnaping.

The necessity of guarding the boys and staying alert to any danger to me makes me feel as if we are living in a prison. I would not, for instance, feel safe going to a store with both boys, for I could not protect both of them simultaneously. Michael spoke to Jason yesterday, standing on the lawn in front of our house. Michael said, "You know, I'm big enough and smart enough, I could take those boys again any time I wanted to."

I am torn between wanting to believe that horror could not happen another time and remembering again, as I have so many times since March, that I *knew* that Michael was going to do something frightful that Saturday morning and I walked away from the house without thinking of protecting Alex and Chris. No matter how excessive my protection seems now, I could not bear it if I failed to take some precaution and they were kidnaped again.

We have been talking intently in the office about the probable necessity of closing. I think more and more strongly that my original hope, that Michael and I could live peaceably in the same town and share in the care of our children, will not be fulfilled. I continue to hear from Clarence—who for all his unreliability is my only source of direct information about Michael's current state of mind—that Michael's rage at me remains at a high level. He is quoted everywhere in town as saying that I am not a good (competent) doctor.

John and the hospital board have clearly given their support to Michael. He was allowed to see patients at the hospital within eight hours of his return, to the anger of many nurses who pointed out that if one of them had done what Michael had done she would certainly not have been welcomed back to her job with open arms. To the extent that the hospital is willing to go along with Michael's demands that there be a choice between supporting Michael or me, it may become impossible for me to sustain a medical practice here. And now, more than ever, I need an assured income.

Paul also advises that I move away, and he is urging that I consider a move as geographically distant from Michael as possible. Paul now believes that Michael will devote himself to harassing me—Oscar tells Paul that Michael's stated concern for the children is no more than displaced anger at me, that Michael is in fact very little concerned with the children's welfare. Everything so far would suggest that Michael is quite willing to risk harm to the children—indeed to be self-destructive—in his efforts to hurt me.

If it is true that the only hope for the children and me to find some degree of safety and peace and security is to move away from here, then we four at the office who have worked so hard to build a practice devoted to the health needs of families must bring ourselves to a decision about closing. Our devotion to our work and to each other has been heightened by the months of shared trouble. It will be difficult for us to part.

My major concern now remains with Alex and Chris. Mary writes that she is happy at camp, and Jo reports from her counselors that Mary seems content and is a steady leader in her cabin group. Jason sees Michael occasionally, mostly when Michael has some threatening message for me. For all his talk about his devotion to his children, Michael has not once talked to Jason about Jason, nor has he invited Jason to have a meal with him, go for a drive, go to a movie or share any activity that might begin to reunite Jason and him.

Alex is much less spontaneously talkative with me or with anyone about himself and his absence than Chris. He has begun to have temper tantrums of raging stubbornness whenever he believes that Chris has been given some unfair advantage. The tantrums often end with Alex destroying something of his own that he values—today he dismembered the sunglasses that he had asked me to buy for him yesterday. It is sad that he feels so bad about himself. He is also asking for all kinds of help with dressing, eating, and playing that seems in imitation of Chris and is certainly out of keeping with Alex's six-year-old competence. Chris often acts as Alex's mouthpiece, as if both of them knew that Chris was more likely to get adult attention and response than Alex. I expect that of the two Alex will have a much longer and much more difficult process of rebuilding his good sense of himself—I always feared that Alex would be the more damaged by the kidnaping, since Chris has always been so distinctly Michael's favorite.

WEDNESDAY, JULY 21: A day in court for all of us, two days ago. Michael seems to have much more ability than I to make things happen in court, at least around the issue of his father-right. In response to his demand for instant rights of visitation, the judge has ordered two hours per week, the meetings to take place in the county courthouse in the presence of an armed sheriff. The first meeting took place yesterday. At the end of the hour Alex and Chris told me that they did not want to do that again.

We have decided to close the practice. I am so strung out with the time and energy demands of safeguarding the children that it would be impossible to sustain my work at a pace sufficient to support the office expenses and earn myself a reasonable income, even if we were supported by the good-will of the hospital.

The trips to and from the day-care center take two hours of each day. The visitations in the courthouse require my absence from the office for two full afternoons each week. The hours that I spend devoted to Alex and Chris—both for their protection and for their healing—deplete my energy resources. A friend, doing research on divorced mothers, reminds me that I am not alone in this dilemma—it is not unusual for women immediately after a divorce to be torn between their critical need to earn an income and the demands of family care and postdivorce adjustments in housing and other living arrangements.

Barbara and Meg will probably also move away from this town. Both are nurses and don't want to work here in the face of what Barbara calls "assholeism." Planning to close the practice is a complex matter—we need to allow for our own relocation and for a safeguarded transfer of our patients to the care of other doctors. In addition, it is not clear whether Michael has foreseen the possibility of our move. It is my impression that he is devoted to ruining my income, but that he may not have thought through to the consequences of my move away from here.

The divorce seems stalled on dead center. That is, of course, entirely to Michael's liking. He lives in a rented room, drives a car with an out-of-state license, boasts that he can keep bank accounts out of state so that no creditors can attach his money. The longer he is able to delay the greater is the possibility that my juggling act will fall apart, or that I will fall apart. Michael is postponing the divorce by insisting that he wants to claim custody of the children before a judge. The two attorneys insist that the matter be settled out of court. They do not want to anger the judge by asking that he make a judicial decision about custody. Paul keeps warning me that I may lose some measure of the judge's good-will and consequently the chance for a decision in my favor, if it is I who insist that the custody matter come into court. I am beginning to feel alarmed at the delay, at the impossibility of my moving until the divorce is settled, at the approaching start of school and the need for the children to be relocated by the time school starts.

Chris now seems past the worst of his psychological reactions to the kidnaping. He only shows us a long face and an expression of astonishment when his demands do not take precedence over Alex's. But he recovers from his disappointments with good grace.

Alex on the other hand is becoming much more fierce and direct in his angers. His tantrums no longer end with the destruction of something that he values but with a direct physical attack on another child—Chris, Mary, or a random playmate. They tell me at the day-care center that he rarely has tantrums there—his anger seems to be roused only in situations that involve Chris and another family member. Difficult as it is to live with his anger, I am glad that he is able to express it. I can imagine that for the four months of the kidnaping he thought he was quite unable to say when he was hurting, for fear of losing what little of Michael's care and attention he could get.

Chris has a favorite litany, at moments when he and I are alone together. "Tell me again all the people who were looking for me when I was away." He wants to hear that Mommy was looking, and Mary and Jason, and then every friend that he knows and loves.

FRIDAY, JULY 23: We have decided to close the office. We are scheduled to take an office vacation for the month of August. I am assuming, or hoping, that the divorce can be brought to an end before August is over, and that we can then inform patients in an orderly manner that the office will not reopen. Each of us in the office has gone through some process of grieving. I think we all continued to hope to the very end that there would be a way of salvaging our work, some magical event like Michael's departure from the town.

Paul feels urgency, on the basis of his conversations with Oscar, about the need for the children and me to leave town, at least temporarily, for our safety. I have arranged to rent a vacation cabin at a lake that is close enough to Jo's day-care center to allow the boys to stay there. They are loved there and can be both in contact with each other and separated in rooms and with different caretakers so that Alex does not constantly feel in competition with Chris, as he inevitably does with me. I think that we will all

feel better when we have left this town and our sense of imprison-
ment.

The town remains full of rumors about my neglect of the children. Michael hired a detective to follow me, Paul has learned
from Oscar. He was instructed to "get something" on me with
respect to my sexual behavior or drug or alcohol addiction. He
returned a long report—after following not only me but friends
who have visited me and the others who work in my office—saying
only that I work hard and sometimes drive too fast on the high-
way.

Too bad that the report cannot be posted on the hospital bul-
letin board; certainly Michael's slanders are noted with all due
attention. Meg, Barbara, Ann, and I even considered suing
Michael for slander and for our consequent loss of income-earning
ability, but Paul tells me that nothing that a husband says against
a wife can be considered slanderous in the legal sense.

One consequence of my being investigated by a detective is that
patients have been further frightened of me. A doctor in the next
town, presumably aware of the questioning about drug use, has
told several patients not to come to seek my medical care because
I was "under investigation for the misuse of drugs."

WEDNESDAY, AUGUST 4: We have taken up residence in a three-
room cabin on a lake within commuting distance of Jo's day-care
center. Meg and Molly will spend some time with us here. My
days are filled with work preparatory to closing the practice and
with the negotiations toward a divorce agreement. There is an
enormous sense of relief in being out of that town and away from
the constant pressures engendered by the parallel threats to my
personal safety and to the boys' security. At the same time I am
filled with dreads about running out of money, being able to
move and get the children settled down before school starts, finding a new job.

I am not even certain at this point where we should move to.
My inclination is to consider the various state laws on parental
kidnaping. If it should happen again, I would want to be living
in a state where my legal position is the most advantageous. Paul

continues to counsel me to move very far away, arguing that only in that way can I become free of Michael's harassments. I, on the other hand, am drawn to Minneapolis, where I have friends and where Jason attends school.

I have also been toying with a totally different alternative. If, as is sometimes argued, it is better for children to be with one adult than to be endlessly pulled from one pole to another, and if Michael is determined to pull them apart because his need to hurt exceeds his concern for their well-being, should I simply go away and leave them with him? I know that I could not surrender them to him and stand by, knowing how he is with them. That was, after all, the primary issue of the divorce. But I could go very far away, lose my identity, disappear from their lives.

Am I only gasping from the endless pain, the hate thrown at me constantly, the chronic uncertainty that we will be allowed to live out our lives free of threat and harm? That may be. But I also am horrified at the idea that it takes two arguing parents to pull children apart; since Michael apparently will not stop his grasping at them, and since the courts will always allow him access to the children and will always question the worth of my relationship with them, I am tempted to believe that I hold the key to release them from years of being torn apart.

I consider the notion with care. I draw out what little is left of my savings, plan that I would drive far away and find work as a live-in housekeeper, change my name, live out my life as a person-in-my-own-right, starting anew, all old ties broken. It is, of course, only another form of suicide—I have convinced myself that I cannot end my life.

I begin to talk about that plan. Jason, Jo, Meg, and Janet all argue against it. I know that they are trying to help me, to comfort me. I am not so sure that they would tell me if they thought the plan had any merit as far as the children are concerned. All say that I *must not* abandon the children to Michael. All have seen him with the children and argue that his harm to them is in direct proportion to the amount of time that he spends with them. Even, they argue, if the courts allow him to remain in contact with them, even if they must spend some weekends and some weeks in the summer with him, they will be the less harmed by that for spending most of their time with me. What, I ask, if by some fluke the courts award their custody to him? I am told firmly that that cannot happen, that if it did there would be an appeal, that many people who have seen and heard him with the children would testify on behalf of the children.

My strength ebbs and flows. I put aside my thoughts of running away when Paul calls to say that he thinks we are approaching an agreement. Oscar thinks that Michael has come to a point of being willing to end the divorce negotiations if I will sign over to him the bulk of the property, including especially the house that I wanted to preserve as the children's home. Now that the die is cast for our move, that home is no longer an issue except for its value in money. Paul and my parents are angered that Michael will have garnered for himself such a disproportionate part of our property. I will gladly turn my back on that if in trade there could be some respite from personal harassment of me and the children.

No, I will not run away. My children are gathered to me. I will move to Minneapolis to be near Jason, because he needs us as we need him. I will pull together another place to live and another job and will support the three little children by my own wit and energy. Our household has gained a gigantic measure of peacefulness, care, and kindliness. I *have* gained something for the children, and for myself, by having ended that long and mistaken marriage. And, ironically echoing my thoughts on the eve of deciding for a divorce, in only sixteen years, when Chrissy is grown and launched, I will be thoroughly divorced from Michael.

Unmarried motherhood is going to be good for me!

EPILOGUE

When a marriage has as its most central successful focus the rearing of one or more children, family ties, no matter how broken or distorted, go on until the children are old enough not to need day-to-day parenting. My marriage contained two sets of contradictory binds that made it particularly difficult for me to escape.

Relatively short-term marriages can be broken more easily than very long marriages because the habit patterns between spouses are not so well established. Friends have said to me, "Of course my own marriage only went on for five (or seven or ten) years; we did not have such a long history together." Short-term marriages, on the other hand, are likely to have still-young children whose very vulnerability and dependency makes them the target of contention. Fathers who are inclined to threaten departing wives by a child-custody challenge are more likely to do so when there is a child too young to be questioned about parental preference. By contrast, long-term marriages, which do have years of established habits, are not so likely to have a small child whose custody can be disputed with such terrible pain. My marriage had both long-term habits and a very young child, making it especially difficult to break.

In addition, my marriage was notably restricted by the binds of social convention, by the knots created from two different sets of convention-intense arrangements: we had the expectations of a marriage contracted in the 1950s, with all the rituals of wifely

and motherly duties that time implied, and added on the expectations of parents of the 1970s, with the implied hope of a new
father-child relationship. I worked so hard to help Michael learn
to enjoy fathering, hoping as other women did that a real attachment based on caretaking could replace the old patriarchal father-
right of ownership. I discovered too late that the attachment was
real enough but that it was grafted *onto* the patriarchal father-
right. It would be difficult right now, I think, for the most earnest
father to disown the male right of property ownership of his
children, since that right is so ingrained in legal and social conventions.

I have continually tossed in my thoughts my two explanations
for the events of this divorce, and especially the events of the kidnaping of the children. Either one can understand what has happened as the unravelings of a singular, exceptional, extreme form of
marriage between two particular people, Michael being wounded
male and mother-hater in the extreme, or one can see these events
as informative and in many ways typical of the contemporary
Commonwoman experience of divorce. Not all divorces are as
painful as this was. On the other hand, I daily hear stories of
child kidnaping, husbands punishing wives by extraordinary
means, continuing and exasperating harassment of former wives
by men who feel rejected, child-custody challenges now taken
seriously by the courts—all done in a mood that is in some ways
a consequence of and in some ways a reaction to the contemporary
women's movement.

The marriage ended on August 29. Michael agreed to a divorce
settlement, coming at last to the end of his notion of reconciliation.

It is sobering to contemplate what I risked, and lost, when I
became a wife. In all the years of that marriage I worked hard to
build security for my family, a professional career, a comfortable
home. The man who was my husband could and did take from
me—with no protest from the courts—my savings, the properties
in which I had invested, my job, my home. He could even
threaten to take my children away. I willingly submitted to Mi-

chael as the wife he owned and mothered the children he owned. I allowed the loss of my rights.

Clearly, my vision of a divorce in which we might sever marriage ties but also strengthen the attachment bonds of our family was impossible. If Michael could not own me he could not cherish the family bonds of parenting nor even the friendship bonds of our shared experiences.

Alex and Chris are still working through the meaning of that long trip they took with their daddy. I genuinely hope that when they are much older they will be able to think about that trip as an adventure they shared with each other, a special bond between them. For now, the scars are still deep and sore.

Chrissy has fared the more easily of the two. Since we moved away from our small town and our constant and chronic worry about a new kidnaping, Chris has stopped his night frights and the bed wetting that had become a new problem for him at the age of three. He has lost his expectation that he will always be judged in the right when he has a disagreement with another child but not his expectation that he will always be loved, no matter what his transgressions.

Alex continues to have gigantic fits of anger, now directed less at himself and more at others. They arise only when he perceives that Chris has taken some small advantage over him and when there is a third person present. He never has tantrums in school and does well in his schoolwork. When he came back in July he had forgotten much of his school-related learning, including his burgeoning ability to read. Now he seems ready to catch up with his agemates.

One night at bedtime, three months after his return from the kidnaping, Alex began to talk about some of his unhappiness while he was traveling with Chris and Michael. While Chris was being read a bedtime story, Alex burst into tears and said, "Everyone loves Chris and no one likes me." He said that every night he is awakened by gigantic animals that come to his room and frighten him—he named several zoo animals—elephants, tigers, and leopards. Asked if he went to see some zoos on his trip, he said that they had, and added, "My daddy always carried Chris, and they talked to each other, and I could never hear what they were saying. And there was no one to hold my hand when we saw the animals at the zoo."

"Did your daddy hold Chris when you were walking other places, not at the zoo?"

"Yes, and he would never listen to what I was saying. I would ask him to take me back to my mommy but he wouldn't hear me. If he heard me he would get very mad and tell me to shut up."

It seems likely that six-year-old Alex needed to be careful for those four months not to show his anger lest he lose what little attention he could get. If he can now begin to talk about his feelings, perhaps he can discard his acting-out tantrums, a healing that is already beginning to happen. Oddly and significantly, however, both Chris and Alex have a return of symptoms (night frights and tantrums, respectively) in the twenty-four hours before they go to visit their father.

We are luckier than some others who have lived through kidnaping by the father; some of those children or mothers or fathers have died. But let no one presume to say that those events are not deeply disturbing for the children who are kidnaped. That exercise of paternal property rights must be seen as deeply harmful to children.

I am aware, these days, of a far deeper appreciation of the tiny pleasures and pains of living than I could ever allow myself through all the years of that marriage. Needing no longer to justify—even defend—the compromises I had made that proved so hazardous for my children, I now can take the luxury of examining the texture of our lives in close detail. What I find is a degree of trust and empathy between the children and me that creates an almost palpable glow in the peace of our home. We do argue, struggle, scold, and complain; but underlying all of that is a firm sense of well-being. Perhaps most telling: the children no longer seem to need to draw themselves into dreadful competitions with each other—as if they know now that in the microcosm of their world at home there is no favoritism, no "scarce resource" of attention or affection to be angled for. Despite the pain of the last year, our family has survived—indeed, is thriving and well. I am glad, for us all, for the courage of my decision.

As we were finishing dinner last night—Jason, Mary, Alex, Chris, and I—we talked about violence and anger.

Alex said, "My dad let us have guns but *we* don't play with them now—they have violence in them."

Chrissy wiggled in his chair with eager delight. "Yes, when I grow up I'm *really* going to be Mighty Mouse and stop all the fighting in the world."

Jason grinned. "Chrissy, I think maybe you could do that."

Mary put down her glass, looking thoughtful. "Maybe when we go visit Dad, if we keep him company, he will lose his violence."

Ceres' Proserpina said the same thing about Pluto.

APPENDIX

Parental kidnaping—especially kidnaping by fathers—is now occurring increasingly often. On the following pages I have summarized the present legal status of parental kidnaping, some remedies for help if such a kidnaping occurs, and some current views on the prevention of this attack on the personal security of children. Because mothers are traditionally less well regarded by the law than fathers and are therefore more in need of information that enables them to pursue independent action, I have addressed the following remarks primarily to women.

LEGAL STATUS OF PARENTAL KIDNAPING

Because the kidnaping of a child is a way of *taking* the custody of that child (acting outside of the law), it is important to view parental kidnaping in the perspective of the current legal conventions regarding disputed child custody.

The notion that any person has a "right" to a child seems contradictory to the idea that we are a nation without slaves. The right of one person to another is an attribute of possession. The problem of parental rights arises most acutely when a child's parents are quarreling, separating, or divorcing. With whom shall the child live and by whom will the child's care be provided if not by both parents together?

In common law, child custody was "the right of the parent incident to his duty to care for his child. The father was entitled to the custody, earnings, and services of his children as a result of his obligation to maintain and educate them."[1] In modern times, the father-right to this entitlement has been based on maintenance and education *through the provision of money.* Courts have ruled, for instance, that a father legally separated from the mother of a child cannot be found guilty of kidnaping that child from the lawful custody of the mother, because "a father cannot completely divest himself of the obligation to support his children by a separation agreement; this being so, the right to custody which is incident to the obligation to support cannot be so completely contracted away as to make the father guilty of kidnaping."[2] In other words, whenever a man assumes a paternal responsibility to support a child he acquires a legally protected "right" to that child.

Until about 1900, when the monetary (income-producing) value of children decreased, it was generally assumed that if parents separated the father had the right to custody of his children. Since that time courts have generally favored the "maternal presumption" and the "tender years" doctrine, legal terms for the assumptions that mothers are generally better caretakers of young children than are fathers and that very young children especially need the care of their mothers. The father-right remains embedded, however, both in law and in social expectations; even adult children are often expected to submit to the authority of a father who provides financial support or even college tuition. (Mothers who are financially able to support their children often assume the entitlements of the father-right.)

The "maternal presumption" and the "tender years" doctrine have recently been challenged as sexist and therefore unthinkingly discriminatory, both toward women who have been assumed to be instinctively parental and toward men who have had a lesser claim to custody. The sexism of these assumptions usually hurts women by pressuring them to take custody of their children when they may prefer not to do so. Some men have claimed, on the other hand, that their rights to child custody have not been properly attended to.

In fact, if fathers' claims to child custody were now given equal weight to mothers' claims (as by some toss of a judicial coin) fathers would again have a *greater* likelihood of taking custody of their children, since they also still have the father-right entitlement based on financial support. And the tossed judicial coin is not so unlikely a simile as one would wish; many family court observers report that judges make custody decisions on very uncertain grounds, dislike making such decisions because the reasons for contested claims seem so unclear to them, and often overturn each others' decisions on appeal. The child's attachments may be claimed as a reason for a custody decision, but attachments to parents cannot readily be measured or compared.

The parental and judicial dilemma with regard to child custody and parental kidnaping is especially acute now because of the swift rise (10 percent per year for the past five years) in the divorce rate. Between one-third and one-half of all children growing up in the 1970s are expected to spend an average of six years (one-third of their childhood) living with only one parent.

Changing views on sex roles, on the meaning of paid employment to both men and women, and on family responsibilities and privileges have resulted in an increase in the number of fathers who spend time taking care of their young children. In some social circles fathers are *expected* to be participating parents. Some children are even cared for more by their fathers than they are by their mothers. Although these latter instances are now often publicized and celebrated, they are probably not much more frequent than they have ever been, and for the most part mothers still do the major share of child care. Adult-child attachments are readily developed, however, consequent to even a minimal amount of care taking. As a result, there are more and more breaking marriages in which fathers claim that they, like mothers, are attached to their children and wish to argue a claim to custody.

In addition, the recent progression of women's self-respect has probably resulted in an increased number of divorces in which the wife proclaims simply that she wishes no longer to be married. This is in contrast, for instance, to divorces by wives charging infidelity or failure to support. When a woman does request a divorce on the grounds that *she wishes no longer to be a party to marriage,* her husband is likely to feel angrily cheated of the wife/servant/mother promised by our traditional mythology about family life and may feel justified in seeking to punish the woman who has so cheated him. The prospect of a division of property can intensify anger about loss of possession of the wife.

The changing attitudes of the law with regard to child custody by fathers, and the uncertain grounds with which custody decisions are made by judges, give men an opportunity to satisfy their attachments to their children and punish their wives at the same time. Legal opinions and statutes with regard to parental kidnaping similarly encourage men's punishment of wives by extra-legal *taking* of child custody.

Parental kidnaping is often done with the intent to transport the child to another state and to sue for legal custody in that new state, hoping to overturn an earlier judicial decision. Alternatively, some parental kidnapings are done with the intent to avoid a judicial decision altogether, in the hope that the kidnaping parent can live secretly and never be found by the other parent. Kidnaping constitutes a grave infringement of the rights of the child to safety, security, and the ability to predict her or his location in space and affection.

The Federal Kidnaping Act[3] explicitly excludes parental kidnaping, as do the kidnaping statutes of many states. Kidnaping by a nonparent is often done for ransom and is therefore more likely to be a crime against rich parents than against poor parents, involving large sums of money. Penalties for nonparental kidnaping have been severe; not long ago it was proposed that the death penalty should be used for kidnapers-for-ransom. Parents have been excluded from kidnaping legislation because it has been assumed that ransom will not be involved, because of "the natural desire of parents to exercise control and custody over their children,"[4] and because of the view that the kidnaping parent has no "unlawful intent."

For the most part the courts have been more concerned with the rights of parents than with the rights of the kidnaped child.

Sometimes that concern is directed to the rights of the parent with legal custody who has lost the child, and sometimes the concern is directed to the "natural" rights of the kidnaping parent.

Some generalities that illuminate the legal regard for parental kidnaping are the following: (1) Before there has been a legal separation or divorce, and before a temporary custody determination has been ordered by a court, either parent is assumed to have an equal right of access to a child; if one parent takes a child away from the other parent (even with a stated intent to conceal the whereabouts of the child from the other parent), there is usually no legal remedy. (2) A custody order granted when one parent and/or the child is out of the state (called an *ex parte* order) may be overlooked by law-enforcement agencies or the courts, on the grounds that the court had no jurisdiction over persons absent from the state at the time of the order. (3) A custody order granted in a marital separation may not have the force of a permanent order granted at the time of a divorce, and sanctions against parental kidnaping may be considered not applicable to separated parents. (4) Custody orders are always subject to reconsideration, pursuant to the demonstration of "new circumstances." New circumstances may be interpreted so broadly as to include the mere passage of time. Parental kidnaping has thus, in effect, been encouraged by the law as kidnaping parents are rewarded by being granted a new custody hearing, often with a successful outcome for the kidnaper seeking custody. (5) Parental kidnaping has been further encouraged by the refusal of some courts in some states to respect the judgment of the court in the "home state" in which custody was determined (refusal to give "full faith and credit," in legal terms). (6) Some courts have also refused to apply the "clean hands" doctrine by which "he who seeks equity must do so with clean hands; equity will not condone inequitable conduct by the petitioner."[5] Thus, despite the fact that a custody suit has been reopened through "ruse, trick, violation of a decree, or other misconduct,"[6] courts have been willing to reconsider the decree and not infrequently to award custody to the kidnaping parent. (7) Most laws applicable to parental kidnaping do not deal directly with the problem of kidnaping by an agent of a parent, so that courts have to decide whether kidnaping by an agent is to be considered a more serious offense.

Some of the variations in specific state decisions and statutes are illustrative of the reasoning of legal authorities in this matter. Since laws change and judicial opinions drift (sometimes in several directions simultaneously) no attempt has been made here to summarize the current legal status of parental kidnaping for each state.

In some states, parents are exempt from kidnaping statutes.[7] There are three possible reasons for this exemption. First, such statutes are said to have "no application to contests between parents for the possession of their children" and are not meant to "punish their natural guardian for asserting his [sic] claim to the possession and control of them."[8] Second, "The conventional justifications for parental immunity are preservation of the family unit and maintenance of societal peace."[9] The argument here is that to allow a parent whose child has been kidnaped to complain to the court about the kidnaping would weaken family solidarity. This line of reasoning certainly assumes that marriages are kept together by force and overlooks the assault to family solidarity already accomplished by the kidnaping itself. And third, kidnaping by a parent is said to be "less reprehensible" than kidnaping by a stranger since "the child's security is protected by the cloak of parental affection, and the . . . anxiety of the parent having lawful custody is greatly reduced from what it would be if a third person had taken the child."[10] Case histories of parental kidnapings amply demonstrate parental anxiety for the safety and security of the child who has been kidnaped and significant psychological and/or physical damage to the child in many instances.

In some states, parents who kidnap their own children are immune from liability if they believe themselves to be acting to protect the child from harm or neglect,[11] and claim they did not know that they did not have full right to the child's custody.[12] The effect of both these exclusions is to give the advantage to the kidnaping parent in excusing his or her actions, since each claim is easy to make and difficult to disprove.

Parental kidnaping is a felony in one state.[13] It is a felony in a few other states only when the child is exposed to risk of harm, transported out of state, or the act is otherwise qualified.[14] In most states it is a misdemeanor or an offense of similar light penalty.[15] Fines in the case of conviction, for instance, may be as little as $75.[16]

The act of parental kidnaping is regarded with a certain lack of seriousness. If the punishment were of some considerable magnitude, there would more likely be a noticeable deterrent effect. Many parental kidnapers may be so driven by rage, however, that they would risk even a major punishment. Similarly, the kidnaping deterrent available in some states of a court-ordered bond to be posted prior to a child-parent visitation may have little effect on an angry parent determined to kidnap. A more practical consequence of the punishability (seriousness) of the crime of kidnaping relates to the availability of help in searching for a fugitive parent. The willingness of state law-enforcement agencies to search for the kidnaper, and the possibility of arranging the return of the kidnaper and child to their home state once they are found, depend on the seriousness with which the crime is viewed; often, little action is taken when the punishment that might be ordered will be light.

In some states, there is also a parental exemption to the kidnaping statute with respect to the kidnaping of an "illegitimate" child "by any person claiming to be its father or claiming a right to its custody."[17]

Although technically the kidnaped child could sue the kidnaping parent for deprivation of personal liberty or some other damage, in practice this is rarely possible. The most common grounds for suit are by the custodial parent for deprivation of *right* to the child or by the state for evasion of jurisdiction. Thus it is clear that the child's rights are of little concern in the courts.

WHAT TO DO IF YOUR CHILD HAS BEEN
OR MAY BE KIDNAPED

I. LOSING

The most dangerous time for any child at risk of parental kidnaping is that period between the beginning of separation or divorce negotiation and the awarding of permanent custody. Before the awarding of even temporary custody, there will most probably be *no* remedy or recourse if your child is kidnaped. Once temporary custody has been awarded your state laws may provide some assistance. Even after permanent custody has been awarded a parent who kidnaps a child may successfully seek another custody determination in another state.

Delays between the communication of an intent to divorce and the first legal steps in the divorce process—usually the serving of papers and the securing of temporary custody of the children of the marriage—create a time of great danger for wives. Husbands can, without significant threat of punishment, inflict on their wives beatings, rape, slander, verbal abuse, and child kidnaping. Husbands who are angry about an impending divorce may do any or all of the above. The requirement, in most states, that neither spouse may quit the household without losing claim to the residence intensifies the threat of abuse and brutality.

Attempts to seek divorce counseling at this point—that is, before the legal process of the divorce has begun—are problematic. It is not clear whether the healing potential of counseling, at this time, can outweigh the increased potential for abuse brought about by the added delay in legal proceedings.

If, therefore, you are in the early stages of a divorce and think that there might be even the slightest possibility that your child could be kidnaped, you should (1) familiarize yourself with the legal statutes and opinions on this matter in your own state through an attorney experienced in parental kidnaping cases, and (2) *guard* your child well. If your spouse is the child of divorced parents, remember that child kidnaping, like child abuse, is often repeated from one generation to the next. Guarding your child might be best accomplished by bringing a friend or relative into your home for temporary assistance, and by quitting or taking a leave of absence from your job.

The services of an attorney are probably essential in the event of a child kidnaping. Knowledge of and experience in the complicated and often devious legal remedies for this sort of kidnaping are probably the first criteria for choosing an attorney. But if there were ever a legal problem that called for compassion, this is it. One is fortunate indeed to have the services of an attorney who is not only competent but also humanly responsive to the tragedy of the lost child. Children's Rights, Inc. (3443 17th Street, N.W., Washington, D.C. 20010) and United Parents of Absconded Children (Box 127–A, Wolf Run Road, Cuba, New York 14727) serve as central agencies for parents whose children have been kidnaped and can sometimes make attorney referrals.

II. SEARCHING

Local Police   Local police often do not want to get involved in a "marital dispute," especially in a small town. Even if you have a custody order, if the father has any kind of loose or nonspecific visitation rights—interpretable as including a period of time without reporting or returning the child to you—the local police will probably try to avoid taking any action until the father and child are out of the jurisdiction of their local area. Sometimes a juvenile or family division of a large city police force can offer special help, such as a request that patrolmen watch for the fugitive's car. You should expect always that the men of the police force will give the benefit of the doubt to a man in a "marital dispute."

In dealing with these agents of the law, I am impressed with the humanness of the system. To someone who is not an attorney, there seem to be surprisingly few hard and fast rules. Individuals respond to individual situations variably, depending on who presents the problem, how it is presented, and the momentary mood of that individual. At its worst, this is a system of influence that responds most readily to those who are empowered by society, a system that harms the powerless most. But at its best it is a system of people, some of whom at least are not dominated by either machines or bureaucracies. Although some police officers (as well as judges and lawyers) bend to the wishes of the powerful, there are others who genuinely care about justice and the rights of the powerless. In any case, it is essential to understand how the system works. Think always about who should speak for you to make your request (you yourself? your attorney? someone personally known to the person from whom you hope to seek help? someone higher up in the system?), and how the request should be made. Remember also that if you ask for help and are told "no" there may be another way to request the same kind of help.

The Sheriff's Office Sheriffs are agents of intermediate jurisdictions—counties come between cities and towns and the state as a whole. It is sheriffs who serve papers, when required, for any matter that issues from the county court. Since most divorces and custody hearings occur there, it is usually a sheriff who serves papers for divorce actions, restraining orders, and contempt proceedings related to divorce matters.

Sheriffs communicate with sheriffs. If a kidnaper leaves a jurisdiction with some business of the county court pending (for instance, the serving of divorce papers, the necessary first step in a divorce) the papers can be served by the officials of any other sheriff's office. Sheriffs also serve and enforce protective court orders. If a restraining order has been issued and served, the local sheriff will often make himself or herself available, on immediate notice, for your personal protection in the event of a threat of violence. (In the larger cities and towns, restraining orders are enforced by local police.) Your protection may depend on a *personal* contact with a named sheriff or police officer.

State Police A "request to locate" is probably the closest present equivalent to a "search for a missing person." An "attempt to locate" is carried out by state police; if it is suspected that the missing person may be found at some address, police of that state will look for the person there. If the person is found the police will give that person some sort of message (such as, your wife wants you to call home). They must do this because they are not empowered to act as detectives in private matters and cannot discover and reveal a person's whereabouts without his or her knowledge. By giving such a message to someone who is running away, of course, they are likely to drive the fugitive on to further concealment.

If there is a criminal charge against the child-stealer (either because the law in your state defines your circumstances of kidnaping as a felony or because of some other charge against the kidnaper), the state police of all states jointly will be notified by a computerized notification system that the kidnaper is to be searched for. Often, although not always, any person who comes to the attention of the state police for any reason will be checked routinely; this is especially true for drivers of cars registered outside the state in which they are driving. If the kidnaper is not traveling by car or if you don't know the make and year of the car and the specifics of the registration or if a new car is purchased and registered in a new state, this whole network is nearly useless unless the fugitive commits some offense that brings him or her into the hands of the state police. Roughly half of the cases I have been told of in which a kidnaper has been successfully located through any official law-enforcement agency have involved this use of the state police network for a criminal charge.

In the realm of important crimes (like stealing property) parental kidnaping is usually considered a rather minor offense. The problem arises, then, of whether the kidnaper, once located, can be brought back into the jurisdiction of the state in which the offense is a crime (extradited). It may be difficult or even impossible to convince state authorities—both in the home state and in the refuge state—that the crime is of sufficient magnitude (or sensitivity) to warrant extradition, which requires legal paperwork and the expense of transporting the found criminal back to his or her home state. Sometimes it is possible to arrange for extradition if the state is promised that some private person—for instance, you—will pay the transportation costs. Without an arrangement for extradition, it is possible that the kidnaper may not even be held long enough after discovery for you to go and get your child.

The FBI   Generally, the FBI will have nothing to do with cases of parental kidnaping. The FBI is, however, the only law-enforcement agency other than state police that has acted successfully to locate and return stolen children. Their search-and-find mechanism is probably more active and more likely to succeed than any other in the country, although it is far from what one would hope.

Presently proposed federal bills (H.R. 2965, 4486, 13134, introduced in the House of Representatives by Charles E. Bennett of Florida) seek to amend the Federal Kidnaping Statute so that parental kidnapers are no longer excepted. If one of these were passed, kidnaping by a noncustodial parent would be a federal offense and would call for investigation, apprehension, and criminal prosecution by the FBI, the U.S. Justice Department, and other authorities. The punishment for parental kidnaping would be reduced to a fine of not more than $1,000, or imprisonment of not more than one year, or both.

When FBI assistance is successfully gained it is usually because someone has been able to convince a local FBI official that there are some grounds on which FBI action is warranted—that familiar process of knowing the "right" person and presenting the story in the "right" perspective to someone who becomes personally invested in the safe return of the kidnaped child. Use of the Fugitive Felon Act,[18] in states in which parental kidnaping is unlawful, allows the FBI to search with an "Unlawful Flight to Avoid Prosecution" warrant.

Private Detectives   If a parental kidnaper has disappeared and it is not possible to get some law-enforcement agency to search, one can consider the use of private detectives. Unless you know that the kidnaper has gone to a single location, there is probably an advantage in working with an investigative agency that can cover several different locations simultaneously. Using a private investigator is very expensive. Charges are generally from $15 to $25 per hour plus expenses. Two or even three investigators may need to be on duty around the clock to keep a fugitive under surveillance until a kidnaped child can be rescued.

Private investigators can, among other things, make inquiries from official agencies whose information is generally not publicly available. When investigators are local residents, who know, and have some influence (of trust, money, or power) with other local residents, they may be able to get such ordinarily secret information as forwarding addresses from post office employees, automobile descriptions from the motor vehicle bureau, and billing and charging information from utility and credit-card companies. Private investigators may also spot-check any place where the kidnaper might go. This can be expensive, especially if it is necessary to have the fugitive followed once found; it requires at least two investigators in two cars (one to follow, one to report to the office that the fugitive has been sighted).

They can also observe the schedules and habits of the kidnaper once he or she has settled. Anyone who is in hiding is likely to become aware of a surveillance. Some places are easier to watch than others—a secluded well-to-do home or a protected suburban neighborhood can be quite inaccessible to a stranger, for instance. If surveillance is possible, the written reports from the agency can be quite detailed and may be helpful in planning how to rescue a stolen child.

Only some private detective agencies will act in parental kidnaping cases. Some have an established policy that they will search for and observe the missing child but will not assist in a rescue. An individual investigator may be personally more flexible about this than official company policy recommends. Again, the most vigorous assistance comes from people who have become invested in the fate of the child.

Two questions are raised with regard to the use of locator agents and "self-help" (see section on Fetching) for the retrieval of kidnaped children. First, does self-help retrieval by the parent who has lost a child increase the likelihood that the parent who kidnaped the child in the first instance will do so again? Current estimates (failing a comprehensive statistical assessment) suggest that a kidnaping parent will repeat his or her act in about one-third of known cases. It is believed, however, that the incidence of a second kidnaping is *not* related to the means used to retrieve the children. That is, whether the children are found and returned through legal processes or through the use of self-help, the incidence of second episodes of kidnaping will be related primarily to the psychology and personal circumstances of the kidnaping parent.

Second, do judges look unfavorably on parents who retrieve their kidnaped children through the use of private detectives and other self-help measures? The answer in a specific instance obviously depends on the specific jurisdiction, court, and judge involved. In general, however, it has been the experience of parents of children kidnaped by the other parent that judges are tolerant of the use of self-help measures to retrieve a child *if it can be shown that every available legal process had been exhausted.* The advice of your attorney, who will know the habits of the judges likely to consider your case, will be paramount in your decision about these matters.

The Press It is occasionally possible to get the attention of a sympathetic reporter (often a woman reporter) at a newspaper. Ordinarily, however, newspapers are not willing to print the kinds of information—names, descriptions, and a telephone number to call if the kidnaper is seen—that would be of real assistance in rescuing the child. And in any use of the press there are serious questions about the disadvantages of publicity—the prejudice of a criminal suit, the effect of public knowledge on the personal reputations of the persons involved, the possibility of a reporter or editor printing a story that is inaccurate or biased in a way that might induce strangers to protect or conceal the kidnaper, and the intrusion of curious strangers into one's personal life.

Feminist newspapers offer a different sort of public notice. Women constitute the great majority of service employees. If only one in one hundred of the women who had contact with a kidnaping father had read a feminist newspaper, and if only a few of those remembered the notice they had read, recognized the child and the father, and were willing to make a collect phone call to the mother, that still offers a significant resource of help.

The cost of this sort of publicity would include charges that some feminist publications might make for publishing a notice and the telephone bill for collect calls, many of which would be false leads.

"Finders" I heard about private individuals who consider themselves to be "finders." These services cost money and there is no way to evaluate the potential usefulness of the services contracted for. There are, for instance, people who are not detectives but who hire themselves out to make telephone calls, follow up all the small possible leads (many of which prove ultimately to be false), and try to outthink the fugitive. Included in this group are private citizens who for one reason or another know a good deal about cases of kidnaped children, some attorneys who have handled similar cases, and a handful of people who have discovered that they have some intuitive and calculating talent for this sort of work. One hears about them by word of mouth.

The Federal Passport Office The United States Passport Office (in the State Department) will keep on file a copy of your custody order or restraining order that specifically forbids the removal of the kidnaped child from this country, will refuse to issue a passport to your child, and will notify you of the address provided for your child in the event that a passport is requested. This protection does not apply to exits to Canada or Mexico.

Birth Registries Another government bureau that cannot help search for the fugitive but can forestall concealment is the birth registry office for the city or town in which your child was born. Your child's name could be changed, but not if you specifically request that that not be allowed. If you talk personally to someone in the registry office you might even get notification of any request for copies of your child's birth certificate, such as might be required for school registration.

Schools Your child's school office might notify you of a request for copies of your child's previous school records.

Parent Locator Service (P.L. 93-647, Title IV-D, Section 453 of the Social Service Amendments of 1974) This new federal policy is, at this writing, not yet able to proceed with swift accuracy to find a fugitive but may become more useful in the future. It provides for the use of federal records (of the Internal Revenue Service, Social Security, Veterans Administration, and "all state and federal files") to locate parents who are in arrears in child-support payments. Administered by the Department of Health, Education, and Welfare, Title IV-D is entered through the clerk of the federal court in your jurisdiction.

III. FETCHING

Detention   If there is any reason for a law-enforcement official to stop the kidnaper, and *if* you can be notified of the detention, you may be able to rescue your kidnaped child at that time. If a criminal charge is filed (either a state or a federal charge), you can arrange for your attorney to be informed when the kidnaper is found and detained. This is an uncertain procedure unless you are confident of your contacts with the police. If the criminal charge is through the state and you are not able to arrange ex-tradition, the kidnaper may not be held long enough for you to go and rescue your child.

If you are instrumental in recommending a chain of action (such as a criminal action or a child-abuse charge) that may result in the kidnaper's being jailed or fired from his job, you may have brought your child back to safety but at a cost of even greater anger and resentment and a greatly increased risk of continued harassment, perhaps even another episode of kidnaping.

If you hope to rescue your child through a process of detention it is essential to understand that you must be prepared for the possibility of a lengthy custody hearing in the state in which the child is located. The Uniform Child Custody Jurisdiction Act,[19] which requires the refuge state to respect a custody decision made in the home state—thus discouraging "custody shopping" from one state to another—has been adopted by only a few states.[20] In all other states it is likely that the court of the state in which the child was found will be willing to hear the custody contention; if you are a stranger to that state, you may be at a disadvantage in that legal proceeding.

There is no national network of child-abuse agencies; there are only agencies for the individual states. If you know where your child is and you suspect that she or he is living in a potentially abusive situation, you may be able to request that the child-abuse agency for that state investigate the situation. You may, of course, appear at the time of the investigation; if you have been awarded custody in your home state you may be able to take the child home with you, or you may have to go through another custody determination in the state where the child was found.

Professional Child Snatchers There are people who can be hired to act as parental agents to take a child away from one parent and return that child to the other parent. Some will do this only when the hiring parent is present on the scene; some will not touch the child but will do whatever has to be done to restrain the kidnaping parent; some will do the whole job. Since such persons put themselves at risk of criminal charges, they are usually somewhat odd, to say the least, and often simply hired thugs or hitmen. In all my months of questioning I never heard of a woman who would do that job, nor did I hear of anyone that I felt comfortable about hiring.

The dilemma is simply this: is it worse for the child to continue to be held in concealment by the fugitive or to be rekidnaped by the other parent? I know of no way to answer that question. I do know that I myself could not have hired a professional agent to rekidnap my children.

Such agents can be found fairly easily through that network of parents whose children have been kidnaped. Attorneys also may have easy access to that sort of person. Costs quoted to me ranged from $1,000 to $5,000.

Self-help The hiring of a professional child-snatcher falls under the heading of what lawyers call "self-help," meaning to go outside the formal channels of legally sanctioned agencies. I decided that I had as good a chance of rescuing the children safely and securely if I went myself with friends, rather than hiring strangers, and that I incurred much less risk of danger or fright for the children. What I describe here as self-help involves only the use of amateur help and not paid strangers.

What is needed is a small group of people: one or two strong men or women to distract/restrain the kidnaper, a cool-headed driver, a familiar person to pick up each child, and as many additional people as might be needed for planning and for psychological support. While the safety of the child is a primary consideration, the safety of the self-help team must also be considered.

IV. KEEPING

Methods of preventing a second kidnaping are essentially the same as the methods that would prevent a first kidnaping. Once an episode of kidnaping has occurred, however, a second episode becomes likely.

Trying to live amidst a threat of parental kidnaping is like living in a prison without walls. It is worrisome to be anywhere exposed with the child, to let the child go outside unattended, to allow the child to go anywhere with anyone except you. The intensity of your parenting bond can increase almost unbearably when you are the only person you can trust to safeguard your child against such a terrible threat.

Some schools, some camps, and some day-care centers are familiar with this problem and have worked out protocols to protect "never-the-father" children. You can increase their ability (and your own) to protect your child by talking with the local police and leaving with them a copy of your custody order (if you have reached that point in your divorce negotiations), so that they are prepared to respond quickly to a request for assistance. They may, however, not respond unless they have a great deal of legal paper, such as copies of the visitation schedule, a current restraining order, and so on.

If there is more than one child at risk of kidnaping it is best to separate them whenever possible when they are not in your direct care. A kidnapable child exposed in a public place should, for safety, have at least two persons with her or him at all times. Physically holding the child in one's arms at any moment of danger is both the most likely protection and the most dangerous solution if a potential kidnaper is prepared to use violent means.

One of the most worrisome problems in the protection of kidnapable children is the risk of danger to those who are willing to help a mother guard her children. Anyone who is willing to be violent to an extreme degree will either succeed in kidnaping the child or in severely wounding the child and/or her or his protectors. For this reason no self-help plan of protection can ever be fully adequate. If there are legal restraints that can be used to retrieve a kidnaped child it may be better to let the child go than to risk significant personal injury to the child and/or to the child's protector.

Some states offer more legal protection against personal kidnaping than others do (see footnotes 7, 13, 14, 15 of this Appendix). Some states prohibit a parent's taking a child in custody away from the residence of the other parent. If your state allows you to move away, you should investigate the laws and judicial opinions, with regard to parental kidnaping, of any state you consider moving to.

HOW CAN PARENTAL KIDNAPING BE PREVENTED?

In discussions of the problem of kidnaped children with women, the question of prevention constantly recurs. The following proposals have arisen out of these discussions.

I. LEGAL MEASURES

Three legal measures, already proposed, may serve to deter parental kidnaping. The federal bill reversing the existing exemption of parents from kidnaping prosecution would make parental kidnaping a federal crime, require the use of the FBI and other federal agencies on behalf of kidnaped children, and threaten kidnaping parents with significant punishment.[21]

Adoption in all states of the Uniform Child Custody Jurisdiction Act would remove the temptation of suing for custody in any state other than the child's home state, where the most information about the child's welfare and past and present family circumstances is known. Removal of the present legal encouragement to take a child to another state for a custody hearing might therefore serve as a deterrent to parents likely to kidnap. The "Full Faith and Credit" Bill, H.R. 10977, introduced by Representatives John Moss and Donald Edwards, would mandate every state to honor custody and visitation decrees from other states. It is federal legislation equivalent to adoption by every state of the Uniform Child Custody Jurisdiction Act.

A fourth legal, procedural solution seems more likely to decrease the expectation of parental kidnaping. It is proposed that every child be assigned one primary guardian at birth. Given the current high divorce rate and the known need of children for a secure and continuing attachment to at least one adult through the early years, this is a realistic possibility. The guardian would in most cases be the child's mother, in the expectation that the mother will provide most of the child's care in the early years. In exceptional circumstances, and by petition of both parents of the child, a man might alternatively become designated guardian for a newborn child.

If the divorce occurs before the child reaches adolescence, there would, then, be no expectation that parents would dispute a child's custody. While a procedure to petition for change of a child's designated guardian might be designed to be heard in the courts, such a petition should be forbidden during the time period just before and just after a divorce between the child's parents, thus minimizing the possibility of using the child as a pawn for parents' anger at each other.

II. SELF-HELP MEASURES

The following suggestions have been endorsed by women in the knowledge that our present legal system often fails to protect them in the care-taking aspect of their mothering responsibility.

In contrast to the usual advice to "be careful whom you marry," mothers have emphasized "be careful by whom you conceive a child," or, alternatively, "be careful whom you designate to be

your child's father." It is not easy to judge anyone's trustworth-
iness or potential for violence or revenge. But it is known that
children who have been abused often become abusing parents
and that children who have been kidnaped by their own parents
often become kidnaping parents. Men who treat women like objects they possess are particularly likely to treat children in the
same 'manner and to become enraged at the threatened loss of
any of their possessions.

Accepting money for the support of one's child means, in this
society, that a right of access to the child (the father-right entitlement) is given over in exchange for support. Women who
are not able to be financially responsible for their own children
thus invite a battle for possession of children. The matter is
extremely problematic. Women's earnings are only about two-
thirds of men's earnings, even in equivalent work situations.
Husbands are conventionally older and better educated than
wives, thus increasing earning disparities. Housewives are not
paid for their work. It is thus extraordinarily difficult for a married woman to be certain that she is supporting her children,
except perhaps in the case of those few wives who are employed
in high-paid jobs. It seems, at the very least, to be important
for mothers to understand the conventional legal connection between support and a right of access to the child.

The currently fashionable notion of shared child care puts
many mothers in a doubly difficult situation. On the one hand,
many men need to be coached, encouraged, and taught (if not
coerced) into taking some active responsibility for the care of
their young children. On the other hand, a woman who has
invited and supported her husband's involvement in child care
may find herself faced with a dangerous child custody dispute
or even a kidnaping in the event of a divorce.

For some women, the threat of kidnaping only adds one more
reason to their rationale for remaining unmarried and refusing
to acknowledge paternity for their children.

These are harsh recommendations. They imply that the family
structure of man, woman, and child is now in great jeopardy.
Many would deny this jeopardy, and many more would hope

that the traditional family structure will survive a difficult period. I, for one, would like to believe that both marriage and parenthood can be reasonably, happily, and productively shared by men and women. At present, however, we are in a time of great change and turmoil. Our social and legal institutions are in need of rethinking. Much is in need of repair. But once the changes come, I look forward to the time when men and women, either together or apart, may live with their children, not exercising rights of possession but respecting and honoring each other as individuals.

NOTES

1. H. Clark, *The Law of Domestic Relations in the United States,* § 17.2, at 153 (1968).

2. James R. Mothershead, "The Problem of Parental Kidnapping," *Wyoming Law Journal,* 1955–56, p. 228.

3. 18 U.S.C. § 1201 (1971).

4. Jane A. Lewis, "Legalized Kidnapping of Children by Their Parents," *Dickenson Law Review* 80:305–327, Winter 1976.

5. Ibid., p. 319.

6. Ibid.

7. Arizona (*Ariz. Rev. Stat. Ann.* § 13, 492 [Supp. 1976], District of Columbia (*D.C. Code Ann.* 22, 2101 [1967]); Maryland (*Md. Ann. Code* art. 27, § 337 [1976]); North Carolina (*N.C. Gen. Stat.* 14, § 41, 42 [1966]); South Carolina (*S.C. Code Ann.* 16, § 91 [Supp. 1975]); West Virginia (*W. Va. Code Ann.* § 61–2–14 [1966]).

8. *Burns* v. *Commonwealth,* 129 Pa. 138, 18 A. 756 (1889).

9. Lewis, op. cit., pp. 309–310.

10. Mothershead, op. cit., p. 229.

11. Pennsylvania (*Pa. Stat. Ann.* Tit. 18, § 2904 [1973]).

12. Hawaii (38 *Hawaii Rev. Laws* § 749–56).

13. Colorado (*Colo. Rev. Stat. Ann.* 18, § 3–304 [1973]).

14. Arkansas (*Ark. Stat. Ann.* 41 § 1702 [Supp. 1976]); Connecticut (*Conn. Gen. Stat. Ann.* § 53a–98 [1972]); Florida (*Fla. Gen. Stat.* § 787.03 [1976]); Georgia (*Ga. Code Ann.* 26 § 1312 [1972]); New York (*New York Pen. Law* § 135, 50 [McKinney 1975]); Ohio (*Ohio Rev. Code Ann.* § 2905.04 [Page 1975]); Oregon (*Oregon Rev. Stat.* § 163.225 [1975]); Texas (*Texas Pen. Code* art. 25.03 [1974]).

15. Alaska (*Alaska Stat.* § 11:15:260 [1975]); California (*Cal. Pen. Code* § 279

[West 1970]); Delaware *(Del. Code Ann.* Tit. 11, § 785 [1975]); Kansas *(Kan. Gen. Stat. Ann.* § 21-3422 [1964]); Louisiana *(La. Rev. Stat.* § 14.45 [1974]); Maine *(Me. Rev. Stat. Ann.* Tit. 17A-302 [1976]); Minnesota *(Minn. Stat. Ann.* § 609.26 [1964]); Nevada *(Nev. Rev. Stat.* § 200.359 [1973]); Pennsylvania *(Pa. Stat. Ann.* Tit. 18, § 2904 [1973]); Utah *(Utah Code Ann.* § 76-5-303 [Supp. 1975]); Virginia *(Va. Code Ann.* § 18-2-47 [1975]); Washington *(Wash. Rev. Code Ann.* § 9A. 40.050 [Supp. 1976]); Wisconsin *(Wisc. Stat. Ann.* § 946.71 [Supp. 1976]).

16. Oklahoma.

17. Mothershead, op. cit., p. 233.

18. 18 U.S.C. § 1073.

19. For a copy of the Uniform Child Custody Jurisdiction Act, write to The National Conference of Commissioners on Uniform State Laws, 645 North Michigan Avenue, Suite 510, Chicago, Ill. 60611 (cost $1.00).

20. The Uniform Child Custody Jurisdiction Act has been adopted by California, Colorado, Hawaii, Maryland, Michigan, North Dakota, and Wisconsin. In Minnesota the policy has been adopted by judicial decision but not by legislation. The act seems likely to be adopted in Wyoming, Delaware, Ohio, and Massachusetts. It is being considered in Connecticut, Illinois, New York, New Jersey, and Texas.

21. See "Booklet Serial No. 38, Transcript of Hearings before the Subcommittee on Crime on H.R. 4191 to Amend the Federal Kidnapping Statute," available from Committee on the Judiciary, U.S. House of Representatives, Washington, D.C. 20515.